Be the Pine, Be the Ball

Haiku Reflections on the World of Golf

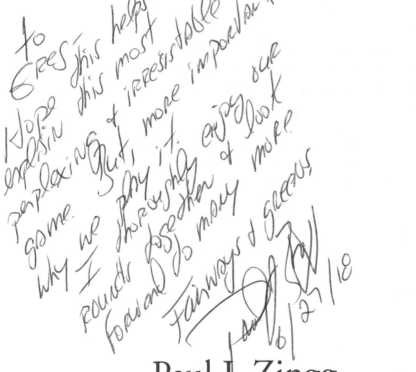

To Greg – this helps explain this most perplexing & irresistable game. But, more important, why we play it. enjoy our look thoroughly & look rounds together & do many more forward to many more. Fairways & Greens

Paul [signature] 6/27/18

Paul J. Zingg

credit: Elizabeth Stevens Omlor

Library of Congress Control Number: 2018903594
ISBN: Hardcover   978-1-9845-1686-2
                   Softcover   978-1-9845-1687-9
                   eBook   978-1-9845-1688-6

Print information available on the last page.

Rev. date: 04/06/2018

To order additional copies of this book, contact:
Xlibris
1-888-795-4274
www.Xlibris.com
Orders@Xlibris.com
774302

CONTENTS

PEOPLE AND PLACE

DISCOVERY AND MEANING

ACKNOWLEDGMENTS

A S I EXPLAIN in the introduction, the number of *haiku*/essays in this book—seventy-two—has meaning both for golf and the forces at work in the universe. For the former, seventy-two is the most common number of strokes constituting a par round on courses around the world. For the latter, seventy-two is both a significant number in mathematics, science, religion, and economics and a "master number" in numerology representing wisdom, balance, and introspection.

Seventy-two is also my age. Although I did not set out with that goal or connection in mind for this book, I came to realize as the book developed that what I was writing was as much an exploration of the relationship between *haiku* and golf as it was a meditation on my own experience with this game. The "journey" of the book paralleled my golfing journey because it sharpened my awareness of the appeal and promise of the game and strengthened my understanding of my place in it. To be sure, this place is not on the same plane as many of my golfing heroes—Francis Ouimet, Ben Hogan, Arnold Palmer, Tom Watson, Seve Ballesteros, Annika Sorenstam—but it is within their framework of respect for our shared passion and quest to find purpose and joy in it.

It has also been a journey with wonderful company. It has stretched from the caddy yard at Essex County Country Club in New Jersey, where my uncle Joe Lucking introduced me to golf, to the trophy case at the Merion Golf Club, where my name is etched on two club championship plaques. It has taken me to five continents and many of the world's greatest courses across the United States and in Australia, Japan, Canada, Mexico, the United Arab Emirates, Ireland, and Scotland. It has been a journey of place and memory—and people. It is a game made more splendid because wonderful golfing friends and companions over the years have shared their love of it with me.

How to acknowledge and thank so many who have shaped and accompanied this journey? It is an impossible task, an indication of how blessed this journey has been; yet a few folks, both individually and collectively, stand out.

Arnold Palmer and Doc Giffin, Greg Norman and Tom Watson, master caddies Chuckie O'Connell at Tralee and Pancho Thornton at Merion, and Pat Ruddy of Ireland's European Club for their interviews, perspectives, and appreciative words for my writing over the years.

The head professionals at Merion (Scott Nye), Cypress Point (Jim Langley), Monterey Peninsula (David Vivolo), and Blackhawk (Tim Burr and Brian Blake), and the club secretaries at Tralee, Cruden Bay, Muirfield, North Berwick, Killarney, Royal Melbourne, and many other clubs who provided access to their grounds and insights to their history.

My many playing partners at the Canyon Oaks and Butte Creek Country Clubs (Chico, California), the University of California Golf Club (Berkeley, California), Blackhawk Country Club (Danville, California), and the Merion Golf Club (Ardmore, Pennsylvania). My longest and closest friends from these places—David Staebler, Steve Desimone, Ken Lloyd—and both old and new friends such as Mike and Kim Roth, Lin and Lily Weng, Keith and Julie Western, Eric Johnson, and Jerry Hight, all with whom I have traveled to Ireland or Scotland.

The challenge of putting together lists like this becomes more difficult with every name mentioned and considered. I am grateful the list is long yet frustrated it precludes naming all for whom I have deep gratitude and affection. Yet they know who they are and how much they mean to me. Still, there are a few additional folks who need special acknowledgment.

For thirty-six years, I have had an annual match at Merion with my younger brother, Bill. His record in these matches is not too stellar, but he keeps insisting that "this is the year" every time we tee it up. Bill personifies the search for the key to a better golf game but, more importantly, the love of a brother. He is as good and funny a person as I know, and there is no one with whom I look forward more to playing a round than him. I am grateful for this game for so many reasons, but none more so than strengthening the bond with my brother.

Golf also brought my wife, Yasuko, and her two daughters, Sachi and Chiyo, into my life. Yasuko and I met while competing against each other in the Northern California Golf Association Couples Championship eight years ago. Like many Japanese, she is not entirely sure whether a *gaijin* like me is capable of writing *haiku*. Perhaps this is the main reason why I give myself a little cover in this book and describe the poems as *haiku*-inspired. But she appreciates the effort. She is a fine player in her own right with a game and attitude that attract friends everywhere and travel well. The girls are another blessing through this game, and they always ask how the writing is going. I am convinced that they think my effort is somewhat brave. I know that they are extremely kind, diplomatic, and beautiful. Oh yes, there's Rui the dog, a twelve-year-old yellow lab. He thinks my *haiku* are brilliant. He also thinks I provide the best doggie treats ever.

When I first read Michael Murphy's *Golf in the Kingdom* in 1972, I was intrigued by the promise of Shivas Irons, the golf pro at the Burningbush Links where the golfing action takes place, "to come away from the links with a new hold on life." In some small way, I hope this book provides readers with a similar experience—a stronger sense of why this game is important to them. I hope too that it leads its readers to appreciate the company that they also have had on their own golfing journeys.

Perhaps, like no other game, golf is both an intensely personal and exceptionally social game. It is a wondrous and worthwhile pursuit that not only reveals so much about those who play it but offers so many marvelous possibilities in the consequences of its pursuit. It is there within the golfer's saying, *Fairways and Greens*, and the delight in knowing that someone has wished you a *fair way* in a *green* setting.

Paul J. Zingg
March 30, 2018

INTRODUCTION

Haiku and Golf

RECOGNIZED AS THE most popular and practiced poetic form throughout the world, written in scores of languages, and composed by kindergartners and nonagenarians alike, *haiku* traces its origins to various forms of linked verse poetry that began to emerge as a literary expression in Japan about seven hundred years ago. By the seventeenth century, the opening three-line stanza (*hokku*) of the older, much longer poetic form (*renga*) had broken free of its host and acquired an identity of its own.

This development was particularly enabled through the emergence of several masters of the shorter poetic style, most notably Matsuo Basho (1644–1694), Yosa Buson (1716–1783), and Kobayashi Issa (1763–1827).[1] Through their elegant language, effective engagement of the reader, and provocative imagery, they established the key elements of the new genre and raised both its visibility and respectability. Basho, in fact, was declared a saint by the Shinto religious headquarters one hundred years after his death and, thirteen years later, also deified by the imperial government of Japan for his contributions to Japanese culture and spiritual enlightenment. By the end of the nineteenth century, the stand-alone *hokku* had earned its own name, *haiku*.

In its most basic definition, *haiku* is a three-line poem of seventeen syllables, traditionally arranged in a 5-7-5 pattern. As in these two classics by Basho. The first is his most quoted *haiku*, regarded as a prime example of demonstrating "eternity in tranquility."[2] The second is among his most examined *haiku,* especially praised for the pattern of its sounds and the deep emotions he felt and conveyed upon visiting an old battlefield.

furu ike ya	Old pond,
kawazu tobikomu	a frog leaps in,
mizu no oto	the sound of water
natsukusa ya	Summer grasses,
tsuwamonodomo ga	all that's left
yume no ato	of ancient warriors' dreams

But even among the *haiku* masters, this pattern was not always followed, especially when a shorter or, rarely, longer poem fit their needs. Over time and across continents, generations of *haiku* poets have not felt constrained by the 5-7-5 syllable pattern either. Part of the reason for this is that what constitutes a syllable or sound unit in Japanese often differs from what may be the case in English or other languages. Yet even in Japan, there is a creative impulse and healthy divide between those who follow the traditional template and those who do not. This is not surprising given the millions of active *haiku* writers in Japan today. It falls then upon other elements of the poem beyond a syllable or line count to reveal the authenticity, sophistication, and beauty of *haiku.* Or as Billy Collins, the former poet laureate of the United States, has said, "A three-line poem with a frog is not necessarily a *haiku.*"

A principal element of classic *haiku* is a reference to nature or some natural phenomenon. In very precise but familiar language, the *haiku* poet invites readers not only to appreciate some aspect of the natural and sensorial worlds but also through intense detail to cultivate powers of awareness and recognition that even the most ordinary moments and elements of our lives are pathways to understanding. In other words, *haiku* aims to have a meditative *and* consequential effect on the reader.

The more closely the reader considers the image or the moment in the poem, the more revealing and meaningful the poem becomes—and the more we are awakened to the world around us.

Traditional *haiku* poems generally but not always have a *kigo,* or seasonal reference. These references are governed by a precise vocabulary that has been developed over centuries. Basho's "summer grasses," for example, is clearly a summer reference, as also would be such items as lightning, cicadas, morning glories, and fireflies. The "frog" in the other *haiku* is a spring reference, along with such words and images as robin, cherry blossoms, thin mist, and melting snow. The *kigo* furthers the precision of the poem and emphasizes how *haiku* relies on literal accuracy rather than metaphor to engage the reader. Nevertheless, contemplation of detail by the reader occasions a very personal, nuanced, and emotional response.

If the essence of *haiku* is brevity of form and the engagement of its readers, another poetic device called the *kireji* further reveals both the amazing complexity of such short poems and the relationships between its images, which often stand in sharp contrast or reversal of each other. Translated as a "cutting word," the *kireji* both divides the *haiku* into two rhythmical, though often contrasting, parts and reconciles the juxtaposition of the images within the poem. It is, in fact, a verbal (when heard) and grammatical (when read) punctuation mark that can often have a startling effect on the beholder. It can occur at either the beginning or the end of the poem ("the sound of water" and "ancient warriors' dreams" are both examples of the latter), but its purpose is the same: to stimulate the reader's or listener's way of seeing through images both vivid and implied.

Although not the first to write *haiku*, Basho became its greatest master. He earned this distinction not only through the structure and subject matter of his work but also through the reflection of Zen Buddhist influence in his *haiku*. Basho brought the highly focused attention to detail that is central to Zen practice—and evident in another Japanese cultural statement, the tea ceremony—to his poetry. And just as his poems communicated his own heightened state of awareness, they inspired those who read or heard them to seek similar enlightenment through intense contemplation of the images he presented. As Basho wrote: "To learn about the pine tree you must become one with the pine and drop your self-centered view."

Considering this statement is, in fact, one of the starting points for this book. For it is an antecedent of one of the most enigmatic directives in golf—"Be the ball."

This phrase is attributed to a 1980 sports comedy film *Caddyshack*, which focuses on the characters at the fictitious, upscale Bushwood Country Club. In one of the opening scenes, caddy Danny Noonan is on the course with Ty Webb, a talented golfer and the son of one of Bushwood's cofounders. Danny is trying to gain Ty's favor, whom he hopes will intercede on his behalf with Judge Elihu Smails, also one of the club's cofounders and the director of the caddy scholarship program. Throughout the round, Danny seeks advice from Ty on life and his future.

At one point, they are standing in a fairway as Ty prepares to hit his approach shot over a lake to the green. He says to Danny, "Let me give you a little advice. There is a force in the universe that makes things happen—and all you have to do is get in touch with it. Stop thinking . . . let things happen . . . and be the ball. Find your center. Hear nothing. Feel nothing."

Ty then proceeds to tie a blindfold over his eyes, takes a swing at the ball, and knocks a wedge about two feet from the hole.

Danny is amazed at what he has witnessed. Ty then encourages him to give it a try himself. As Danny stands blindfolded over the ball, the following dialogue occurs:

Ty says, "Just relax. Find your center. Picture the shot. Turn off all the sound. Just let it happen. Just be the ball. Be the ball. Be the ball."

Ty pauses as Danny readies the shot. "You're not being the ball, Danny."

Danny answers, "It's kind of hard when you keep talking like that."

Ty replies in a whisper, "Okay. I'm not talking anymore. Be the ball. Be the ball. Be the ball."

Danny takes a swing—and dumps the ball in the lake.

"Be the ball" is one of the entries that can be found through an internet search for "golf quotes." In fact, that request will generate 19.4 million responses in half a second. A somewhat more refined search for quotes on the mental aspects of the game will yield 1.3 million hits.

The number of quotes is staggering to consider, but among the themes that can be identified within them are a few that strongly connect Basho and Ty Webb, *haiku* and golf. These are the power of visualization, the importance of playing within one's own abilities, and understanding golf as a mind/body exercise.

The key to these perspectives, though, is another. Indeed, it is the heart of the matter whether one aims to "become one with the pine" or "be the ball." This is the cultivation of a "quiet mind," that is, the ability to focus on the moment and the immediate target and to free one's mind from the distractions of multiple (and often competing) swing thoughts, memories of bad shots, the behavior and judgment of your playing partners, and images of all the places on the hole where you do *not* want the ball to go. It is to give oneself to the task at hand, to be in *that* moment, and to resolve to accept—and to learn from—the outcomes of the effort no matter what they may be.

Long before the golf gurus of television's *Golf Channel*, sports psychologists, and a canon of writings on the *inner game* of golf appeared, teachers and masters of the game understood these elements.[3]

"For this game you need, above all things, a tranquil frame of mind." The words of England's Harry Vardon, a six-time winner of the Open Championship with a temperament and a swing that made him the greatest player of his time in the late nineteenth and early twentieth centuries.

"Success in this game depends less on strength of body than strength of mind and character." Spoken by Arnold Palmer, perhaps golf's most beloved player whose influence and admirers transcended the game.

"Golf is a game that is played on a five-inch course—the distance between your ears." So explained Bobby Jones, the game's greatest amateur player, who completed golf's first grand slam in 1930, winning both the U.S. and British Amateur and Open championships. He emphasized this point with another observation: "You swing your best when you have the fewest things to think about."

Jack Nicklaus, eighteen times a winner of professional golf's Major championships and about whom Jones admiringly said, "He plays a game with which I am not familiar," understood exactly what Jones meant about focus. "There is no room for negative thoughts. The busier you keep yourself with the particulars of shot assessment and execution, the less chance your mind has to dwell on the emotional."

And then the perspective of Nick Faldo, the most dominant British player since Vardon and the winner of six Majors among forty professional tour victories worldwide: "Visualization is the most powerful thing we have."

There is no evidence or admission that any of these players reached this remarkable consensus on the mental game through Zen training, *haiku* reading, or psychotherapy. Rather, through self-assessment and experience, they appreciated the enormous demands of a game wherein success largely depends upon the ability to play with a "quiet mind" and to exorcise confusion and negativity from the task or shot at hand. What Sam Snead surely had in mind when he said that "Of all the hazards, fear is the worst."

For to accomplish such awareness is to accept one's limitations and, in fact, to achieve a certain liberation from them. It is to embrace Bob Rotella's famous declaration that "golf is not a game of perfect." It is to be focused on the moment and engaged in a process of continuous improvement—therefore building both confidence and sanguinity.

Through focus and precision, visualization and imagination, we can begin to appreciate the connections between *haiku* and golf. Clearly, Basho and the other *haiku* masters were not thinking about their short games when they opened a pathway to enlightenment through their writings but the intrinsic qualities of *haiku* translated to the inner game of golf because—the poets were thinking about life. And golf, as Bobby Jones observed, "is the closest game to the game of life—you get bad breaks from good shots; you get good breaks from bad shots; but you have to play the ball where it lies." And all along the way, the entire "walk down the fairway of life," as Ben Hogan counseled, "you must smell the roses—for you only get to play one round."

Beyond the authentic imagery of *haiku* and the invitation within the poems to the reader to pause and to become absorbed in the images, especially to strengthen the powers of detailed observation with a related reduction of distractions, there are other aspects of the connection between *haiku* and golf that are worth noting. These particularly include significant parallels in the history of both these human endeavors and the nature of their rules.

As noted at the beginning of this introduction, the origins of *haiku* can be traced to a rich and deeply respected poetic tradition in Japan. The earliest anthology of Japanese poems, the *Man'yoshu*, or *The Collection of Ten Thousand Generations*, was compiled between 686 and 784 AD. Several other major anthologies followed in the centuries to come, including collections that emphasized the 5-7-5 syllabic construction. So by the time of Basho in the seventeenth century, Japanese poetry had been evolving for over a millennium.

Basho arrived at an especially important moment in Japanese cultural history. Under the Tokugawa shogunate, the country had entered a relatively peaceful era due, in no small part, to the political decision to disengage from the outside world. Literacy was expanding, and more popular forms of expression, such as Kabuki theater and woodblock prints, were gaining favor. The spiritual influences, familiar images, simple style, and imitable form of Basho's poems appealed to the public at large and set the stage for an era of great enthusiasm for *haiku*, which persisted throughout the Edo Period (1600–1868) and beyond.

Significant moments and catalysts have also marked the history of golf as the game evolved. Its origins can be vaguely traced to several stick-and-ball games that had become popular in Europe by the Middle Ages. Exactly which of these games most directly influenced the shape of golf is impossible to say. By the late fourteenth century, however, about the same time that the seventeen-syllable, 5-7-5 construction was emerging as an independent poetic form in Japan, a recognizable version of golf (in fact, called *golf*) was being played on the links land of St. Andrews, and apparently being played a lot. For the first written reference to golf appears in an Act of the Scottish Parliament in 1457 prohibiting the activity because it was interfering with archery practice. The latter was identified as more crucial to the defense of the realm than certain "unprofitable sports," golf among them.

But the game could not be denied, and once the royals and aristocracy took to the game, as the records indicate both Mary, Queen of Scots and King James IV of Scotland did, it was hard to contain their subjects' access to it. By the end of the sixteenth century, golf had evolved into something very familiar to today's game. It was played over several consecutive holes on "courses" covering a considerable expanse of land. Recognized early as ideal land for this pursuit were the extensive strips of sand-based, thinly cropped turf lying between the sea and a town. In fact, linking sea and town—links land.

In the mid-eighteenth century, about the same time that the *haiku* masters had established the framework of their craft, golf experienced additional defining moments in its development. Foremost among these were the appearance of a set of rules to govern the game and the determination that eighteen holes constituted a regulation golf course.

The former occurrence is attributed to the Gentlemen Golfers of Edinburgh, later to become the Honourable Company of Edinburgh Golfers with their home at Muirfield. In 1744, the gentlemen set forth thirteen "Articles and Laws in Playing at Golf" to govern the game for their five-hole circular course on the Leith links. These became the basis for all subsequent guidelines for the conduct of the game, including golf's primary rule to play the ball as it lies.

The latter occurred on the other side of the Firth of Forth at St. Andrews. Here, the Society of St. Andrews Golfers had formed in 1754. Their golfing grounds included eleven holes, laid out end to end, east to west, along the Eden Estuary from the clubhouse to the far edge of their property. At that point, the golfers turned around and played the holes backward for a total round of twenty-two holes. By 1764, however, the membership decided that several of the holes were too short. Consequently, they were either eliminated or combined with other holes, and the entire layout was reduced to eighteen. Due to the status of St. Andrews as the golfing capital of Scotland, all other courses soon followed suit, and eighteen holes became the world's standard.

Coincidentally then, three centuries ago and half a world apart, the basic framework and direction for both *haiku* and golf had been established. From humble and provincial origins, the poetic form that Basho and the early masters shaped and the game that the gentlemen golfers of

Leith and St. Andrews refined have since translated into true global phenomena.

A list of just the Western poets in the twentieth century who have turned to *haiku* for some of their work is a genuine who's who of poetry. Robert Pinsky, Robert Hass, Gary Snyder, Seamus Heaney, Billy Collins, Richard Wright, Sonia Sanchez, Jorge Luis Borges, Lorraine Harr, Robert Spiess, Alexis Kaye Rotella, Elizabeth Searle Lamb, Anita Virgil, Jack Kerouac, William Carlos Williams, Donald Hall, Paul Eluard, Richard Brautigan, Emanuel Xavier, Allen Ginsberg, W. H. Auden, e.e. cummings, Ezra Pound, Joanne Kyger, Anne Waldman, Amy Lowell, Nick Virgilio, Anselm Hollo, John Wills, and Richard Wilbur barely scratch the surface of those attracted to the elegance and immediacy of *haiku*. If, as the American poet and editor Sam Hamill declared, "Basho is the great river of *haiku*," then its tributaries are many and powerful, constantly flowing and being renewed, as new generations discover and embrace this poetic form as their own.[4]

The same can be said about golf. If Scotland is its birthplace and St. Andrews its home, over thirty-three thousand courses worldwide and an estimated sixty-plus million people who play the game attest to the strength of the sport's foundation and its extraordinary appeal. How to explain its appeal, though, is a question that yields perhaps as many answers as there are people who play it. Not to mention the broad reach of the golf "industry" that includes everything from equipment, clothing, and tourism to the golf media, golf-centered resorts and residential communities, golf instruction, and golf-related food, beverages, and health care for both body and mind.

Hogan discovered in the game "a universal language" wherever he traveled. Probably not the vocabulary that Raymond Floyd, a four-time winner of golf's Majors and a 1989 inductee into the World Golf Hall of Fame, had in mind when he quipped "They call it 'golf' because all the other four-letter words were taken."

Other explanations suggest a vivid connection to some of the elements and goals of *haiku*. Tom Watson, for example, has noted that "Confidence in golf means being able to concentrate on the problem at hand with no outside interference." He explains further that "No other game combines the wonder of nature with the discipline of sport in such carefully planned ways. A great golf course frees and challenges a golfer's mind."

For Hale Irwin, one of Watson's contemporaries and a three-time winner of the U.S. Open, the hold that golf has on its players is rooted in the game's intense focus on an individual's struggle with the course, par, and, ultimately, himself. This makes golf "the loneliest of sports." And for Gary Player, who formed the Big Three of professional golf with Palmer and Nicklaus in the 1960s, golf was essentially "a puzzle without any answers." But therein lies its appeal—a timeless and ordered quest for a sense of one's place in a game that withholds perfection but offers enlightenment.

When all is said and done, though, it is hard to find better observations about the game's nature and attraction than those offered by Bobby Jones and Arnold Palmer. "No one will ever have golf under his thumb," said Jones. "No round ever will be so good that it could not have been better. Perhaps that is why golf is the greatest of games. You are not playing a human adversary; you are playing a game." And Palmer: "Golf is deceptively simple and endlessly complicated. It satisfies the soul and frustrates the intellect. It is at the same time rewarding and maddening—and it is without a doubt the greatest game mankind has ever invented."

If *haiku* is one of the world's greatest forms of literary expression and golf one of the most challenging ways men and women satisfy their need for play and recreation, what would it look like if they were combined? What insights and enjoyment could the former bring to the latter? What discoveries about the history, nature, and appeal of the game might emerge from this fusion? What light might this joining shed on why so many choose to play this game, as elusive and frustrating as its mastery might be?

These are the fundamental questions that this book seeks to answer.

The book is organized into three sections around three themes:

- *Landscape and Memory* focuses on the history and both the collective and individual memories attached to golfing landscapes and elements and the larger geo-cultural scene that hosts and frames them.
- *People and Place* emphasizes specific courses, or features of courses, and key people who have played important roles in shaping the history, culture, and character of the game.
- *Discovery and Meaning* explores those aspects of the game that underscore its appeal to those who play it, including its role as a pathway to self-discovery.

Undoubtedly, there is some overlap among these categories. The Old Course at St. Andrews, for example, is a *place* that is firmly etched within both the *landscape* and *memory* of the game. For the most part, though, distinctions can be drawn among the categories, and they provide, as good as any, a way to explore and organize key themes.

Each section or theme contains twenty-four *haiku* or *haiku*-influenced poems for a total of 72. This is a meaningful number in golf since 72 is both the most common number of strokes for a par round and the number of a holes in most professional tournaments. The number also has important connotations in mathematics, science, religion, economics, and numerology. The latter identifies 72 as a "master number" that promotes enlightenment and introspection. Indeed, goals of the *haiku* poets.

Each of these poems is accompanied with a short essay that provides some context for them. The goal of the essays is to assist readers in recognizing *haiku* as a sound, albeit unconventional, approach to strengthening their appreciation of golf and an awareness of their place in the game. The essays are neither prescriptive nor geared only for readers who are familiar with *haiku*. They do not dictate a single way to enter the poem. Rather, as is a central tenet of *haiku*, the essays invite engagement with the poem and acknowledge that the reflections that may flow from their encounter may be as varied and valid as those who read and consider them.[5]

With few exceptions, the *haiku* in this book follow the traditional 5-7-5 syllable construct. The few that do not still reflect the authenticity of the *haiku* form. Similarly, like much of contemporary *haiku*, especially outside of Japan, not all of these poems follow the classic framework with *kigo*, *kireji*, and subject matter rooted in the pastoral. As such, they reveal that the essence of *haiku* is much more than a nature sketch within an absolute syllabic pattern. They represent, as the American *haiku* poet Jim Kacian affirms, "a wide-ranging, emotive, capacious genre capable, in the right hands, of expressing anything a poet might wish to convey."[6]

What they all possess, however, is brevity, precise language, avoidance of simile and metaphor, and focus on a single moment or setting in time. Yet there is often a broad sweep, past and present, forming their larger narrative. To the extent that each *haiku* draws its readers "through the keyhole of its details into the infinite" is the extent to which it both satisfies an essential requirement of the form and succeeds as a story and a meditation.[7] Although contemporary *haiku* can look different than its classic expressions, this is more an expansion of the traditional form than a rejection of it. In the end, the realm of *haiku* has broadened, further underscoring the energy, vitality, and urgency of this extraordinary poetic genre.

About one-fourth of the *haiku* and essays are accompanied with illustrations drawn by Elizabeth Stevens Omlor, a children's writer and artist who lives and teaches in northern California. Simple, often whimsical, these grayscale pen-and-ink drawings focus on a key element of the *haiku* or a point made in its companion essay. Their purposes are to draw attention more fully to the *haiku* and/or text and to enhance and enable the reader's engagement with them. No less so, the illustrations also aim to delight the reader on their own.

Through these *haiku* and the structure of the book around its themes, essays, and illustrations, the reader may develop greater attentiveness to the joys of golf and a deeper awareness of his or her place in the game. It is to reach the kind of mindfulness and focus that Uejima Onitsura (1660–1738), a contemporary of Basho, said we are all capable of achieving in this *haiku*:

ume wo shiru	truly to know plum blossoms,
kokuro mo onore	needs your heart,
hana mo onore	and for you to be the flower

Be the pine. Be the ball.

LANDSCAPE AND MEMORY

1

Listen

The club strikes the ball,
it leaps ahead on its flight—
listen to the sound.

ESTHETICS IS A branch of philosophy that explores the meaning of beauty and its expressions in nature and art. Golf is a rich subject for this discipline in that it engages an aesthetic lens on so many levels. Clearly, the design of courses and their settings, both the actual landscapes of the courses and their surrounding environments, compel golfers to consider what is beautiful and pleasing. Architects debate the relationship between strategic design elements and the enhancement of natural settings. Players, for example, appreciate both the history and timeless features of the Old Course and the charms of the ancient town of St. Andrews, which hosts it. Similarly, said the American golf architect Pete Dye about another top 10–ranked course in the world, "Merion is not great because history was made there. History was made there because Merion is great."

The golf swing, of course, invites rhapsodic treatments by the game's teachers through magazines, the *Golf Channel*, and pricey golf academies. These gurus compel golfers to spend countless hours standing in front of mirrors or viewing themselves on videos as they contemplate the question "How does my golf swing look?" These endeavors, though, often seem more focused on what is *beautiful* than what is *effective*, what is *aesthetically pleasing* than what is *individually appropriate*.

This *haiku* focuses on three physical elements of the game that transcend how well one plays the game or where. These elements are intrinsic to the inner beauty of the game and, as such, are accessible to anyone.

First, feel or touch. That is, the touch of the club in one's hand and then the sensation that occurs at the moment of impact when the club strikes the ball. For many who teach and play the game, how one holds the club—that is, how the club rests in one's hands and how much pressure is applied—is where a good swing begins. And just as surely, the feedback one gains from impact is a gauge of how good that swing actually is.

Second, the sight of the ball in flight. This flight is not glimpsed immediately, of course, because the ball has left the club instantaneously at impact and is well on its way toward its target (or thereabouts) before one progresses far enough in the swing to look up and see where the ball is heading. What one witnesses at this moment can be the stuff of delight or despair—and every emotion in between as the ball sails and/or rolls on its journey. The outcome of this journey can be the crucial test of the quality of one's swing and temperament, but it is also evidence of how this game, perhaps like no other, so seamlessly combines skill and chance, knowledge and serendipity.

Third, the sound of impact. To paraphrase Yogi Berra's advice on studying baseball – "You can observe a lot just by watching" – in golf *you can hear a lot just by listening*. Yes, hitting the sweet spot on the club produces instant audio affirmation for you and anyone else within earshot that solid contact has been made. But so much more. The sound of a persimmon-struck ball is not just a distinctive *thwack*. It is an echo of the game's history. The crunch of an iron compacting a ball off the firm turf of a links land fairway is not just unique and satisfying. It affords spiritual connection to some ancient striker on perhaps those same grounds. The swoosh of the full swing not only pinpoints its highest speed, but it also affirms that you have brought intensity to the task.

When one is aware of these senses, one is so much more open to the possibilities of a game that cannot deliver perfection but can provide joy every time it is played.

Broom

In the late summer,
the broom's black pods burst open—
a bygone strike sounds

T HERE MAY BE no sight on a golfing landscape that more beautifully signals a links land location in the British Isles than the gorse and Scotch broom in bright yellow bloom in early spring. These low-lying, evergreen shrubs have a broad native range in Europe extending from the northern United Kingdom to Portugal and east from Ireland to the Ukraine. They thrive in sunny regions, usually on dry, sandy soils at low altitudes. Although introduced as a hedge and border plant in other areas of Europe as well as the Americas, Australia, New Zealand, and South Africa, they are regarded as an invasive species that can create havoc among other plant communities, and by no means exempt, certain human communities as well—like golfers.

Covering hillsides, lining fairways, and, often, overhanging bunkers, both plants have both ornamental and sentimental value, especially when planted in regions outside of their natural habitat. The United States Golf Association, for example, acknowledged these uses in the first volume of its *Bulletin of the Green Section* published in 1921 as a guide "to promote the betterment of golf courses" in America. Along with tips on combatting crab grass, locating bunkers, and designing hazards, the USGA pointed out how these plants added "atmosphere" to a golf course by introducing an element reminiscent of courses in Scotland. The governing body for golf in the United States, however, did not warn of the harm that these shrubs could do to a player's score. They are simply no place where a golfer wants to hit a ball.

Although both plants share certain physical properties such as green shoots, seed pods, colorful flowers, and dense growth patterns, gorse presents the greater threat to a player's game—and body. This is because the plant is taller and thicker than the broom varietals and covered with sharp thorns. When fully mature, these one-inch spines can penetrate even the thickest clothing.

Neither spiny nor as dangerous to the physical well-being of players who come in contact with gorse, Scotch broom is further distinguished from its cousin in another rather charming and contextual way. This is the sound that the plant produces when its green legumes turn black in late summer and burst open in the hot weather. The sound is an audible *crack* that reflects the force of the explosion propelling seeds from the parent plant.

Hearing this sound for the first time—especially experiencing a scatter-shot succession of these eruptions in rapid order—can be both surprising and confounding. But listen carefully. It is the sound of the native landscape where the broom thrives, and it is the sound of persimmon on balata, a distinctive clap launching a ball over that landscape. What a marvelous game to have a reminder of its heritage and nature within the seed pod of a plant—and the window on the world beyond that it provides.

3

Golf in the Kingdom

This splendorous game,
smellin' heather and cut grass,
facin' hopes and fears.

*G*OLF IN THE *Kingdom*, Michael Murphy's mystical, semiautobiographical account of a young traveler who accidentally stumbles upon a mysterious golfing teacher in Scotland, has sold over a million copies and been translated into nineteen languages since its initial publication in 1971. It has spawned the Shivas Irons Society, an organization whose members combine golf and meditation as a pathway to self-discovery; inspired a sequel, *The Kingdom of Shivas Irons*, published in 1997; and materialized as a Hollywood film of the same title in 2011. It is a book that has been categorized under "golf," "mysticism," and "spirituality" in bookstores and libraries and can be found as readily in sections on sport and self-help as philosophy and metaphysics. It is, at once, both the strangest golf book most may ever read—and the most wonderful.

On one level, at least through the first half of the book, *Golf in the Kingdom* is a delightful recounting of a day in June 1956, when Murphy wandered onto the ancient Scottish links of Burningbush for a round of golf. For reasons "political and arcane," Murphy explains, he does not reveal the true name of this famous course, and this apparent sensitivity to the privacy of the membership helps create a semblance of actual experience that cleverly enfolds the reader into the narrative. The rich feel and flow of Murphy's story sustain the edge of belief for some time, even when we first encounter Shivas Irons, the local pro, turning grotesque arabesques in midair in an attempt to kick a beam several feet over his head. For stranger things than this have surely been seen around a golf course.

The details of Murphy's round with Shivas and a well-lubricated review of the day's events, including a whisky-inspired return to "Lucifer's Rug," Burningbush's devilish thirteenth hole, in the middle of the night, comprise the rest of the first part of the book. Murphy's account of their play and postmortem is filled with ruminations about the nature of golf, including those incorporated in this *haiku*, amply provided by Shivas and three dinner companions. For the most part, Murphy found these remarks enigmatic, obscure—and irresistible. For here was a coded approach to the game with which he was not familiar but fully drawn: centering, true gravity, inner body, higher self, second sight, nothingness in shots, auras around balls, streamers of heart power, golf as journey. Strange theories, thought Murphy, but remarkably organized and undeniably compelling.

The second part of the book constitutes Murphy's attempt to make sense of what he saw and heard in the company of Shivas and the others. It particularly focuses on various passages that Murphy copied from Shivas' journals. It is the part of the book that either loses readers quickly or captures them completely. For herein is where Murphy reveals the ultimate purpose of his book: to present golf as a meditation and as a means to personal enlightenment.

For all the explanations attributed to the pursuit of golf—from exercise to exorcism, attainment to atonement—it is fundamentally a *game.* We play it. We don't have to, but we choose to do so. Like any game, the choice to participate is an expression of perceived needs and benefits that may even be more authentic than the forces that compel us to work. Whereas the latter reflect the artificial imperatives of our socioeconomic environment, from which such "play" as "social tennis" and "business golf" derive, for example, the fundamental decision to *play* is a relatively free one.

Sports represent a particular form of organized, competitive, physical play, but they are no less expressions of freedom or joy than the simplest children's games. The key issue is why we choose to play the game of golf among so many possibilities. The starting point for that answer, according to Michael Murphy/Shivas Irons, is the recognition that golf is something we do for enjoyment *and* self-discovery. It is a means to explore and unlock our human potential. Moreover, it is a microcosm of the world beyond the game wherein the greatest threats to fulfilling its purposes are the failure to live our lives honestly and to fall victim to "the quicksand of perfection."

4

Links Land

Grasses of the dunes
hold the scent of sea and sun—
and the game's allure

THE APPEAL OF links land begins with its unique and timeless physical properties. These vast seaside stretches initially captivate the eye with their raw and savage beauty. Especially for golfers whose regular venues of play have been the manicured acres of country clubs and parkland designs, the scene can be both startling and perplexing. It does not look familiar, and it does not seem particularly inviting for golf.

Yet it is perfect for golf. Perfect, that is, for the game that originated on such land and developed to meet its requirements. For upon the undulating, sand-based terrain of fescue and bent grasses, within the turbulent dunes held tight by sturdy thickets of wispy marram and tall sea lyme and exposed to the fierce convulsions of the sea and sky is a landscape that yields running fairways and fast greens and design features shaped more by the forces of nature than the machines of man. This is a landscape that compels the player to recognize what the elements will allow and to bring skill, daring, and imagination to the task of negotiating it.

It is a landscape as distinctive in its sounds and scents as its looks. The sea, of course, is an omnipresent agent of volume and fragrance. It may roar with frightening intensity or soothe with the gentle rhythm of long, low-breaking waves upon the beaches. Angry winds may deliver the briny air in punishing, wind-borne lashes, or the sea air's sweet mix of salt and chlorophyll may arrive on gentle breezes.

Within such an environment, golf is as much a privilege to pursue as a pleasure. Among the world's approximately thirty-three thousand courses, less than 1 percent can be considered true links courses. And 85 percent of these are located in Great Britain and Ireland. They invite golfing pilgrims to witness the origins of the game and experience the magic of a landscape that is both austere and magnificent at the same time.

Such a place would seem full of irreconcilable contradictions, but that is not the case here. Rather, just as their minimalist designs eschew artificiality, they also challenge the skills of golfers of all rank and ability. There may, in fact, be no golfing landscape that reveals either the strengths or flaws of a player's game so honestly than links land. There is no place to hide a weakness out there because every facet of a player's game will be tested, and none more so than his or her attitude.

Links golf requires patience, imagination, humility, and humor. It requires accepting what the land has to offer, not imposing expectations that emanate from very different contexts and playing habits. The competitive edge—and even more so, the enjoyment quotient—may, in fact, go to the player who embraces the nature of the game here than the one who approaches a links course as just another place to ply the usual game or add another notch to one's golfing belt.

All links courses, to be sure, are not equally grand and great, but they are unique and alluring—distinctive in design, location, character, and, undoubtedly, the window they provide on the nature, origins, and core values of the game. It is especially reassuring to see new links courses opening in recent years to rave reviews for their quality and acknowledgment of the history of the game. Both in the countries of origin for links courses and around the world, these include Bandon Dunes, Pacific Dunes, and Old Macdonald in Bandon, Oregon; Barndougle Dunes and Barndougle Lost Farm in Tasmania, New Zealand; Cabot Links in Nova Scotia; the European Club and Doonbeg in Ireland; and Castle Stuart, Kingsbarns, and Machrihanish Links in Scotland. These new layouts mean that golfers do not have to travel to the ancient courses of Ireland or Scotland to find an authentic links land experience, and most certainly, they affirm that the future of golf will continue to connect to its past—and its soul.

5

Holy Ground

By the water's edge
an ancient ball strike echoes—
a new chorus swells.

STRETCHING EAST FROM Edinburgh along the southern shore of the Firth of Forth is one of Scotland's most picturesque and historic regions. Its coast accommodating long sandy beaches and charming harbors, its heathery countryside embracing market villages and great estates, East Lothian is a land rich in beauty and the memory of its past.

These qualities are evident in often stark and surprising ways. The ruins of Tantallon Castle, the former seat of power of the Black Douglas family, overlook the seaward entrance to the port village of North Berwick from their cliff-top perch. Its massive earthwork defenses and towers are dramatic evidence of a time when the warring clans and factions throughout East Lothian built their castles and fortifications and battled each other and the English. In contrast, Dirleton Castle about five miles to the west, its twelfth-century walls surrounded by gardens and lawns, suggests conditions of peace while the great country houses of Lennoxglove at Haddington and Gosford near Longniddry provide settings of romance.

Never far from any of these landmarks of Scottish history and culture are the several grounds of another. From Musselburgh east to Dunbar along the nearly unbroken stretch of coastal links land and inland from Haddington to Gifford and south to the Lammermuir Hills, the region offers as many and as fine a variety of golf courses as anywhere in the world. Reflecting not only the quality of its twenty eighteen-hole courses but also their place and role in the game's origins and development, East Lothian is truly one of golf's holy lands.

Its closest equivalent elsewhere in the world might be the Monterey Peninsula in the United States. For it was here that a transplanted Brit named Charles Maud, in the vanguard of his countrymen who spread the gospel of golf to North America, designed the area's first nine-hole layout at the edge of the Del Monte Forest. The Del Monte Golf Club opened for play in 1897 and has been the oldest course in continuous operation west of the Mississippi River ever since. There are now nineteen other eighteen-hole courses within a fifteen mile radius of the area's first.

The game's faithful have been congregating on East Lothian's links and heathlands for a somewhat longer time than the pursuit of the game upon the central coast of California. Mary, Queen of Scots reputedly tested her game on the Musselburgh links in 1567, an outing that may have influenced the club's receptive attitude to the play of women. Members of Bonnie Prince Charlie's court did the same in 1745 before embarking on their ill-fated campaign to restore a Stuart king to the British throne. The Jacobite uprising began on a promising note with the rout of an English army at nearby Prestonpans, where the rules for stroke play competition were developed in the late nineteenth century at the club now known as Royal Musselburgh. But seven months later, the Bonnie Prince and his rebel army were annihilated at the Battle of Culloden near Inverness. Charlie escaped to France, where he lived in exile the rest of his life until dying of a stroke at age sixty-seven in 1788. Ironically, he found a nascent golfing culture there that could be traced to Mary, Queen of Scots because of her marriage in 1558 to Francis, the Dauphin of France.

The spectrum of the golfing scene in East Lothian—ranging from the aristocratic environment of the Honourable Company of Edinburgh Golfers at Muirfield to the democratic celebration at North Berwick embracing children and visitors with equal enthusiasm—clearly reveals the variety of the game's expressions. Accommodating octogenarians and adolescents, patrician tastes and plebian means, explorers of its mystical character and pilgrims to its holy sites, it is a game of extraordinary appeal and passion.

Yet as in the attempt to define a nation's "character," likened by the American historian David Potter to a blind man in a dark room searching for a black cat that may not necessarily be there, the quest to discover a common meaning of the game is bound to be an exercise in futility. Better perhaps to heed the observation of Shivas Irons, the mysterious golf pro of Michael Murphy's *Golf in the Kingdom*, that golf is "a game for taking off the seven veils. Never think ye first glimpse the last, for there are aye another six." Through six centuries of golf and a score of wonderful courses, East Lothian still has much to reveal in the landscapes and memories of the game that thrives there.

6

Common Ground

Between sea and land,
the rumpled landscape beckons—
and yields the Old Course.

WHEN SAM SNEAD first glimpsed the Old Course through the window of his train taking him to St. Andrews for the 1946 Open Championship and his Claret Cup victory, he thought he was looking at an old, abandoned golf course long gone to seed. It was a reaction shared by countless first-time visitors to these grounds. No doubt, like Snead, they expected to behold something more obviously grand—or at least something announced more grandly. But there are no arched entranceways to the golfing grounds, no shrubbery arranged to spell out "The Old Course," no high walls with "No trespassing" signs surrounding it (although there is a sign on a boundary of the course that warns: "Danger: Golf in Progress"). The course sits on a landscape where golf has been played for over six hundred years, resting patiently, bewitchingly, unassumingly, between the sea and the town.

Although photographs and prints (such as Alistair Mackenzie's 1924 hand-drawn colored map of the course), articles, player testimonials, and television broadcasts have helped provide a sense of communion and familiarity with the Old Course for golfers all over the world, it eludes true description unless it is witnessed and played firsthand. And once is unlikely enough to appreciate its charms and quirks. Especially for golfers whose domain of play may be the industrially produced acres of modern earthmovers, formulaic designs, and computer-generated modeling, there is little context for the wild, unconstructed landscape that is the Old Course and the brilliance and allure of golfing grounds that have not been transformed from something else.

For what prepared this landscape—and links land courses throughout Scotland—so fittingly for golf was the shaping power of nature itself. Its elements included the primeval crumpling of the earth's crust, the many moods of the sea and winds, and the consequences of the great glaciers that moved relentlessly across this land over several ice ages. The moraines and eskers, drumlins and erratics, and pitted outwash plains that the moving ice left in its slow processional are the features of true glacial topography. It is a coarse and obdurate landscape, spectacularly savage and beautiful, kettled and kamed, untillable, inimitable and irresistible. Perfect for golf.

These forces and circumstances have had an ennobling effect not only on this and other links courses, but also on the local inhabitants who, for centuries, sought recreation upon them. Until the twentieth century, though, the game they played there was more an esoteric passion than a national pastime and far less a global phenomenon. Nevertheless, it is the memory of human interaction with the landscape, not some environmentalist agenda or civic promotion, that commands respect for the Old Course and sustains a cult of exceptionalism about it. For teeing it up at the Old Course not only places a golfer within the memory of this particular place but also within the historical fabric of the entire game.

The magic of St. Andrews is ultimately both finite and transcendent. It is cast in the physical properties of the Old Course and the spiritual bond with its players. It exists in a game that provides an identity for a town and a home for golfers everywhere who play it. And if, as Shivas Irons, one of the great character inventions in Michael Murphy's whimsical novel *Golf in the Kingdom*, observed, we "need a solid place to swing from," it might as well be the common ground of this ancient kingdom by the sea.

7

Spirits in the Mist

Memories are deep
within the dunes and hollows—
spirits in the mist.

ON IRELAND'S WESTERN coast, "where the air is so soft it smudges the words," wrote the Irish poet Louis MacNeice, a stretch of dunes land sits a few miles south of the meeting of the River Shannon and Atlantic Ocean. Architects and players, poets and scribes have long formed a brilliant chorus of praise for what lies there with the turbulent sand hills, desolate beaches, tormenting winds, and fierce sea—Ballybunion.

Invited with Molly Gourday to suggest improvements for the course in 1936, architect Tom Simpson said: "The beauty of the terrain surpasses that of any course we know. Never for one moment did we imagine, or expect to find, such a really great course or such a glorious piece of golfing ground." The great dean of golf writers Herbert Warren Wind took up the beat in an article for the *New Yorker* in 1971. "To put it simply, Ballybunion revealed itself to be nothing less than the finest seaside course I have ever seen." And someone who knows something about links courses, five-time winner of the Open Championship Tom Watson had this to say: "After playing Ballybunion for the first time, a man would think that the game of golf originated here. There appears to be no man-made influence. It looks like a course laid out in land as it was in the tenth century."

The quality of timelessness, which Watson recognized, extends beyond the size, beauty, and untamed appearance of the golfing landscape. Its seven seaside holes in particular fit so splendidly into what nature has provided there that the pioneers of the game at Ballybunion largely *discovered* their presence, not designed them. Indeed, as the brilliance of the Old Course at St. Andrews is due largely to the absence of meddling with its fundamental features, as anachronistic and quirky as some of them might be, the same is true at Ballybunion. As a result, it is a course that commands those who come to visit to look but not touch. For it is a course of exhilarating beauty and no discernible weakness, offering eighteen distinctive holes that can easily be recalled after a round. Ballybunion's memorability rests not only in the way its distinctive topography has embraced and formed the course but also the shot value that accompanies its transit from the first drive to the last approach.

There is also about Ballybunion—and such other Irish courses as Portmarnock, the European Club, Royal Portrush, and Royal County Down—a reflection of the country's larger landscape. It includes such characteristics as wildness, isolation, spaciousness, and a sense of spiritual presence. Indeed, the severe, elemental nature of these courses invites spiritual connection with some distant ancestor of the game who could not resist propelling an object over the beckoning landscapes.

Other spirits abide in these grounds, too. The ghost of Old Tom Morris has been reported wandering the fairways and haunting the rough of Royal County Down. The Vision of Killasheen, a banshee-like creature, can be glimpsed—at the risk of shortening one's life—walking an ethereal bridge that leads from Ballybunion into the sea. The Gray Man, the fairy form of the ancient Celtic storm god, *an fear liath*, exerts his sinister influence through the thick fog that often shrouds these coastal courses. The sheerie can appear anywhere and the ill effects of their encounter—temporary derangement and aimless wandering over the countryside—suggest their particular attention to golfers.

Yes, there are memories in these landscapes and spirits in their mists. They are deeper than what has been recorded in the histories of these clubs and beyond what the eyes can see. But most certainly, they await both resurrection and reverie, the delightful consequence of giving oneself to the game, the elements, and the land.

8

Into the Mystic

In the land of Eire,
between myth and memory,
mystic chords endure

T HAT THE ORIGINS of golf on the sites of some of Ireland's most renowned courses are somewhat hazy is no fault of the game's historians. Rather, it is a commentary on the nature of history itself in Ireland and the general sense that nothing is quite what it seems in this land. For the merger of actual events with spirituality and superstition has influenced a holistic sense of the past that often makes no distinction between what is remembered and what is imagined.

The Irish foundation myth is rooted in the *Lebor Gabala* ("The Book of Invasions"), a twelfth-century monastic manuscript that traces the lineage of Ireland's great families to Adam. Within it, we find Eire, the namesake of the country. She is the wife of Mac Greine, a grandson of Dagda, the chief god of the Tuatha De Danaan. This *tuath*, or tribe, translates as "the people of the [mother] goddess Danu." They arrived in Ireland as survivors of the Great Flood of the Old Testament and spent much of their existence fighting off other invaders.

The defining moments in their history were two great battles fought on the plains before the southwestern mountains of Slieve Mish. Their opponent was a warrior tribe called the Milesians who had landed in a large fleet in nearby Kenmare Bay around 700 BC. Although the Milesians emerged victorious from these battles, they were so impressed with the bravery of their enemy that they agreed to divide the land with them. The Milesians received dominion over all lands above the ground, while the children of Danu retreated to a new kingdom of their own beneath the ground and the sea. It is within these folds of "mother earth" that the descendants of Danu occasionally emerge from caves and sacred mounds in the form of "the little people"—fairies and leprechauns and other such spirits who pester and delight the surface dwellers.

This sense of the divine and ancestral spirits within and upon the land, firmly formed in myth, folk voice, and history, affects all aspects of Irish life, culture, and conversation. And no less so golf—especially when it is a course within view of the Slieve Mish and the influence of the ancient spirits who dwell there.

This is the Waterville Golf Links, located at the far end of the Ring of Kerry, upon the sand hills and strand bordering Ballinskelligs Bay. It was in this bay that grandchildren of Noah had arrived after the flood with the patriarch's command to go forth and repopulate the earth. They were so successful in this endeavor that the Irish have claimed major credit for the rebirth of human civilization after the deluge. One of the heroes of this effort was Ladra, who undertook his assignment with such enthusiasm that the *Lebor Gabala* recorded that he died heroically from "excess of women."

More misery and drama descended on the southwest in the seventeenth century AD with the outbreak of the Civil War in England between the Parliamentary forces of Oliver Cromwell and the loyalists of King Charles I. Facing a ban on their religion yet committed to its practice, Catholics throughout the region found ways to hide their priests and celebrate Mass in secret. Those in the coastal villages like Waterville often trekked out to remote spots along the coastline and concealed themselves from Cromwell's soldiers and spies within the dunes. One of these sites, a deep depression between the tee and the green of the par 3 twelfth hole, aptly named the "Mass Hole," is one of those places.

Today, the twelfth still inspires prayer to handle its challenges. From the championship tee set high upon an exposed dune, it requires a two-hundred-yard carry over the blessed chasm to reach the near circular green. Although only a single pot bunker guards the green, it is hardly defenseless. Any tee shot not gaining the putting surface will careen backward into the holy hollow. Any ball landing beyond the green will be confounded by the tall grass and steep upslope awaiting there.

It is a brilliant hole that underscores the spectacular setting and natural elements of the entire course. Ranging from the tranquility of the par 5 eleventh, which meanders through an alternately pinching and broadening valley of gorse-covered sand hills to a green perched on a tiny mesa to the fierce environment of the nearly six-hundred-yard finishing hole, which is completely exposed to whipping winds and rain off Ballinskelligs Bay, the course impresses and challenges every step of the way.

The eighteenth caps this journey with another Waterville spirit. For overlooking the green and welcoming players after their round is a life-size statue of Payne Stewart, the two-time US Open champion who died tragically in a plane crash in October 1999. Stewart had been a frequent visitor to Waterville, where he prepared for many Open championships. In September 1999, after the Ryder Cup matches at Brookline, Massachusetts, and in appreciation of his affection for Waterville, the membership named Stewart an Honorary Captain of the club. It was the last golf honor he would receive before his death.

The spirits of Waterville are deep within the memories that are formed, recalled, and imagined there. They contribute to a powerful sense of the mystical in this land that Irishman Van Morrison captured in one of his most poignant songs:

"We were borne upon the wind
Also younger than the sun
Ere the bonnie boat was won
As we sailed into the mystic"[8]

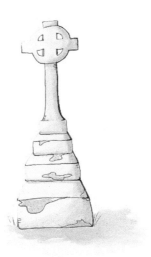

9

Foreboding

Rain begins to fall,
the ancient graveyard whispers—
not here, not today

A ROUND BEGINS WITH many thoughts but a single goal—to get off to a good start. As will be the case for the entire round, the success of the day will largely depend upon the attitude and effort that a player brings to the first tee. Both require a fine balance between acknowledging the excitement of the moment and handling the emotional rush that accompanies it. Indeed, the challenge of the first shot on the first hole—wherever it might be, however familiar it might be, and whomever the company might be—is a uniquely compelling moment for any round and any player.

But there is more to the start of a round than the design, playing circumstances, and setting of the first hole. At one time or another, for example, every course will experience severe weather, and it may descend upon players as they take the first tee. It may accompany them the entire round. But bad weather—a sandstorm in Dubai, a flash flood in Arizona, a squib in Ireland, gale winds at Pebble Beach—is an ordinary occurrence even if it achieves extraordinary ferocity. Storm clouds, rain showers, or temperature extremes should not necessarily deter the hearty or ruin a round if one has dressed for the conditions and adjusted both game and expectations accordingly.

What may be more unnerving, though, are the features of some courses that seem purposefully menacing. They may lead a player to doubt the prospects for a happy round ahead. The names of courses, or the particular areas of some courses, can fuel this unease. What chances for golfing good fortune await at clubs with such names as Nightmare, Hangman, Monster, Ghost Creek, Hell's Point, Purgatory, White Witch, and Devil's Claw? What odds for survival, much less a good score, exist within Hell Bunker at the Old Course or Hell's Half-Acre at Pine Valley or the Devil's Cauldron at Banff Springs?

Yes, what's in a name? But consider these examples where the hauntings, omens, and intimidation factor are truly unique.

As players approach the first tee of the Bethpage Black course in Old Bethpage, New York, they will find this sign: "WARNING: The Black Course is an extremely difficult course which we recommend only for highly skilled players." Dante could not have been more explicit about facing the gates of hell when he wrote: "Abandon hope, all ye who enter here."

An ocean away at the Old Course of Ballybunion on the west coast of Ireland, players prepare to hit their first shot staring at a haunting sight only a few yards away—a cemetery. The hole is aptly named "Tombstones." The scene is all the more unsettling when it is enshrouded with the gray, dense fog that visits these regions. The Killehenny graveyard borders the right side of the fairway for over a hundred yards, so most decidedly, it can come into play. Yet for two obvious reasons, it is not where you want your first ball of the day to go—it is out-of-bounds, and it only welcomes the dead.

On the northeast coast of Scotland above Aberdeen is the ancient fishing village of Cruden Bay. There sits a marvelous links course originally laid out by Old Tom Morris in the mid-1880s. From a vantage point overlooking the course and the beaches of the North Sea are the ruins of the ancestral home of the Errolls, one of Britain's oldest families. This is Slains Castle. For centuries the Errolls battled the Danes and anyone else who challenged them for their lands and power, eventually abandoning the bloody region in the sixteenth century. What remains are the ghosts and the ruins—and imagination. For Slains was the inspiration for Castle Dracula, as envisioned by Bram Stoker who regularly vacationed at Cruden Bay.

In so many respects, what is a distraction for one player may be a fulfilling element of the round's experience for another. The issue is not to deny the rain, or the cemetery, or the castle. It is to *see* and *be* within the larger framework of golf's universe and, of course, that of a particular place and moment. It is to replace fear and foreboding with confidence and providence. Yes, easier said than done but a much more promising outlook than imagining demons and doom determining our days.

10

Fog

Fog shrouded coastline,
Somewhere, someone, smacks a drive—
and pierces the veil

"ONCE MORE THE storm is howling," wrote the great Irish poet William Butler Yeats in a poem to his newborn daughter.[9] "There is no obstacle but Gregory's wood and one bare hill whereby the haystack and roof-leveling wind, born on the Atlantic, can be stayed."

Serious weather is not an anomaly in Ireland. Nor is it isolated to Ireland. But there are elements of location and geology in Ireland that have created a unique set of climatic conditions that have dramatic consequences for golfers.

The Emerald Isle is, first and foremost, an island. Covering about thirty-six thousand square miles, it is roughly the size of the state of Maine, which is no stranger to harsh Atlantic weather either, especially when the cyclone winds of a "nor'easter" sweep in. Although Ireland stretches three hundred miles at its longest and nearly two hundred at its widest, there is no place in the country which is more than seventy miles from some stretch of coastline.

The surrounding waters have two significant influences on the country. First, the tighter range of temperature variations at sea than on land effect a more temperate climate overall with less extremes. Daytime temperatures in the summer hover mostly in the sixties (F) with a nighttime drop-off rarely more than a dozen degrees. Although freezing conditions, including snow, can occur in some northern and eastern regions during the winter months, Ireland affords play year-round.

Second, the Gulf Stream, a powerful current of warm surface water flowing northward from the Caribbean across the Atlantic, passes very close to the coastal areas of southwestern Ireland. Accompanying the Gulf Stream are the prevailing winds that bring the moisture-laden warm air to the shores and inland. These conditions contribute to the vast greenness of the land and such startling sights as palm trees and other subtropical vegetation growing in parts of the lush southwest.

The evil twin of all this movement of air and ocean is that the activity can be intense, fast moving, and unpredictable. Huge depressions regularly form in the Atlantic as the southern winds collide with the much cooler air descending from the northern latitudes. Since Ireland is the first land mass that these depressions encounter as they move from west to east, Europe's last outpost is the weather's first target. The western counties of Kerry, Clare, Galway, Mayo, Sligo, and Donegal bear the brunt of this assault, including the often-thick fog, which arrives on anything but the "little cat feet" in Carl Sandburg's famous *haiku* about the fog in Chicago off Lake Michigan.[10]

Rather, the bone-chilling fog of these regions, the same kind of fog that occasionally descends on Pebble Beach and Bandon Dunes and blankets the Hamptons on eastern Long Island and the shoreline of Cape Breton, is the fog of the Choctaw-American poet William Jay Smith. It arrives "on huge elephant feet" and brings nothing but doom to all that it touches.[11]

In Ireland, though, the sweeping rains and shouting seas are also attributed to sources that defy scientific explanation. For long before writers discovered the moorlands and cliffs, mountains and coasts of

Ireland's western regions, the gods of the Celts and their predecessors gathered and raged there. Aligned with various real or mythological tribes, they emerged from the sea and sky bearing such names as Manannan mac Lir, Gaeth, Balor, and Goll. These are spirits who do not conjure up friendly images of still waters and gentle breezes. Rather, these are gods with an agenda, foremost of which are distressing humans and exciting their imaginations.

It is a brave soul who tempts their powers and a hearty one who finds sport in the harsh weather conditions they command. But in the Gothic twilight of the gray fog and rain, golfers will launch their drives toward an unseen target—and *listen* for its consequences. These are among the moments in this game, both vexing and alluring at the same time, that reveal why it is played.

11

Squib

The squib brings fierce rain,
umbrellas raise against it—
a feeble defense.

SQUIBS ARE BRIEF showers that can occur anytime, anywhere, along the coasts of Great Britain and Ireland. They emanate from seemingly clear skies as easily as overcast conditions and, no matter their origin, rarely last for more than a few minutes. They also strike with different degrees of intensity depending upon the winds that accompany them.

Sometimes the first drops arrive almost apologetically. Large and scattered, they afford a false sense that their falling can be gauged and dodged. Within seconds of the initial sprinkles, however, a torrent of water that might even give Noah pause can pound the uninitiated victims of such weather. Caught unaware and in the open, players may huddle pathetically under their umbrellas, sometimes massing together like a Roman cohort to ward off the incoming arrows with their shields as a protective canopy.

The ferocity and effect of the deluge are fearsome to behold. A field of vision may be reduced to no more than a few yards, although a tantalizing brightness may be glimpsed beyond the curtain of the falling water. Huge puddles instantly appear in the fairway, each glistening like melting silver, the rain drops kicking up frenzied splashes like crowds of fairies exulting at a rock concert.

Squibs are as ornery as the celestial spirits to which they are often attributed. They particularly will treat with contempt anyone who relaxes his guard because of ignorance of their nature or presumption of their passing. As the alliance of wind and rain strengthens, the consequences become more fearful. White caps appear in the shallowest of streams and ponds. Routes to rain shelters achieve greater importance. Golf swings dissolve like Elphaba, the wicked witch of Oz, in the wash of Dorothy's water.

The rain comes down hard, heavy and loud. And then it is gone. Not even a gentle tapering or whispered retreat. It just stops. And we are left to wonder what was *that* all about.

But it lasts just long enough to redefine the concept of par in such conditions and to underscore the Scottish saying, "Nae wind, nae rain, nae golf." Whether bearers of the gentle mists of "soft days" or the furious marks of a visiting squib, the atmospheric activity in these regions makes a distinctive contribution to other commonly felt joys and delights of the game, especially the elements of surprise and serendipity.

12

Garden

Upon the hillside,
a cross in gold surprises—
spirea in bloom.

I NLAND AND UPLAND from the fierce beauty of the Irish sea
coasts, the pleasures of golf in the Emerald Isle also abound. The
Irish interior was once a forest of spectacular density and fertility with
great stands of oak, elm, ash, elder, hazel, birch, and pine covering the
countryside. All this began to change about five thousand years ago,
however, as more sedentary human communities, which depended
upon arable farming and grazing, began to clear the trees in order
to plant crops and create pastures. Axes felled the Irish forests for
centuries, the final blows occurring in the seventeenth century when
British proprietors in Ireland realized enormous profits from the sales
of timber harvests in England, the Netherlands, and other European
markets. Today, less than 5 percent of the Irish landscape is forested,
and much of that is the result of recent reforestation and conservation
efforts.

Several national forests and parks, most notably Killarney in County
Kerry, Glenveagh in County Donegal, and the Wicklow Mountains
National Park centered at Glendalough, provide a glimpse of Ireland's
ancient landscape. There is golf here too, and its play through valleys
framed by thickly wooded slopes of conifer, cedar, juniper, and holly

and along the edges of dark glacial lakes and rushing streams connects players to the memory of the land as surely as the essence of the game. This is not links land, but it is magnificent golfing country all the same. For the game in such settings is no less immersed in Ireland's natural history, spirituality, and mythology than that played upon the seaside cliffs and shores.

The standard for all parkland courses in Ireland is the Killarney Golf and Fishing Club, which traces play along the northern banks of Lough Leane to 1891. Lake country of similar beauty and atmosphere hosts another in Newtownmountkennedy, a tiny village just northeast of Glendalough in the heart of Wicklow, the "Garden County." This is Druid's Glen, which, although only open since 1995, has spearheaded a renewed interest in parkland courses in Ireland. This development both acknowledges the country's golfing heritage and serves as a reality check on the rapid diminishment of available sites for new links land courses in the face of prohibitive costs and stricter environmental regulations.

The site for Druid's Glen is a spectacularly wooded area surrounding Woodstock House, an eighteenth-century Georgian country manor similar to many throughout the region. Perhaps the most famous of these is Powerscourt in nearby Enniskerry. Also dating to the mid-1700s, Powerscourt oversees a thousand-acre demesne, featuring waterfalls, an extraordinary gallery of outdoor statuary, and a series of terraced gardens that are the most impressive in Ireland. The Powerscourt gardens, emulating the formal conventions of their models from seventeenth- and eighteenth-century France and Italy, are demonstrations of affluence, designed to impose order over a vast landscape through transforming nature. As such, they aim to astonish visitors, not merely to delight them.

Druid's Glen seems to have been motivated by the same goal. Like Berckman's Nursery, the land upon which Augusta National was built, the Woodstock estate suggested that a golf course awaited to be fashioned there, not just discovered. Rounded hills, gentle undulations, wooded dells, a granite-walled canyon, and two clear mountain streams provided the designers Tom Craddock and Pat Ruddy with the basic elements to shape their "garden."

The inspiration for the short, par 3 twelfth, though, is more mystical than anything even Augusta National provides. For this is the druids' own garden, a sanctuary of tall trees enveloping a nave-like green, protected front and right by a rock-walled stream. Overlooking the entire scene, about halfway between the tee and the green and tucked among a grove of sacred oaks, are the remains of a druid altar.

It is an absolutely stunning setting yet somewhat compromised with two wholly artificial creations. For standing above the ancient altar with arms outstretched like Leonardo's Christ in *The Last Supper* and wearing a less-than-approving expression on his face is a life-size plastic statue of a druid priest. And sprouting on the face of the elevated tee but unseen unless players look back at the tee from the green is a large Celtic cross perfectly fashioned with dark green dwarf hebes and yellow spirea.

What Druid's Glen represents may be more beautiful than Irish, but it is unquestionably dramatic and memorable. Aside from one too many plastic druids and an occasional berserk horticultural moment, it succeeds as a golf course and a place of immense beauty. It is an experience as much as it is a golf course, where the garden and the game promise delight and surprise.

13

Desert Tracts

In a wild of sand,
verdant fields edge the barrens—
clearings for the game

IN THE EARLY eighteenth century, influenced by the intellectual
energy of the Enlightenment, Western notions of the relationship
between settled human communities and their surrounding natural
landscapes underwent a dramatic change. Previously, two views
dominated. One considered the wild and wondrous wilderness areas
of forests and wastelands that lay beyond the boundaries of town and
village as inaccessible and uncontrollable. These were regions that
evoked curiosity, to be sure, but fear of the unknown severely restricted
their exploration and incursion. Another view emphasized the necessity
of human control over nature. Often taking the form of grand, formal
gardens such as those at Vaux-le-Vicomte in France or Caserta in Italy,
these environments were demonstrations of affluence, designed to
impose order over a large portion of vast landscapes by "improving"
upon a magnificent but notably unkempt, nature.

A third view, though, heralded by such English landscape designers as
Charles Bridgeman, William Kent, and Lancelot Brown, emerged to
reconcile the extremes and to promote a greater sense of seamlessness
between the tamed and untamed natural environments. An instrument
they developed to accomplish this was called the "ha, ha." This was

not the sound of laughter but rather the expression as when one is pleasantly taken by surprise. The "ha, ha" was essentially a sunken barrier, a ditch, for example, instead of a raised enclosure, such as a wall, a fence, or a hedge. Its purpose was to prevent cattle or sheep (or neighbors or wildlife) from crossing from the land beyond the ditch into the cultivated fields and gardens of one's estate. But a marvelous consequence in the removal of physical barriers of view was to create a sense that the tended areas and the surrounding countryside or open space were one and undivided. It was, in the words of the British author Horace Walpole the product of a vision that "leaped the fence and saw all nature was a garden."

There is no category of courses that better demonstrates the engagement of the tamed and untamed in their design than those located in the deserts of southern California, Arizona, and Nevada. Moreover, the variety of these courses illustrates the design extremes that this dialogue has produced. Tom Fazio, who has fashioned more courses listed in the most recent *Golf Digest* ranking of the top 100 courses in the United States than any other living architect, reveals this range in his body of work.

At the far end of the spectrum that reflects the impulse to control nature is Shadow Creek, a course that has been labeled by some as "the seventh wonder of the golfing world." Located just a few miles north of the Las Vegas Strip, it is a course that looks and feels as if it was airlifted from the Shenandoah Valley of western Virginia and dropped intact onto the floor of the Mojave Desert. Casino magnate Steve Wynn commissioned Fazio to design the most spectacular golf course that money could buy and then spent $47 million to accomplish the task. The course opened in 1989. Fazio returned in 2008 to oversee a major renovation of the course to the tune of another $17 million.

Importing over 20,000 trees and shrubs and the fertile soil to sustain them, Fazio completely transformed the flat barrens and desert scrub into rolling hills and canyons where every square foot of the 350 acre site—every creek, lake, garden, hillside, and waterfall—is completely fabricated. There are glimpses of the Sheep Mountain Range through the mature flora and man-made forest of the course but little hint otherwise within the grounds that this opulent oasis is surrounded by a vast, hard-baked, barren landscape. The view of the desert, in fact, is blocked by a perimeter berm constructed with three million cubic yards of native desert soil that had been excavated and shifted from the original site. This feature is the ultimate anti-ha, ha statement. Altogether, Shadow Creek is a surreal experience as much a testament to what a brilliant architect can do with unlimited funds as the notion that nature can actually be improved through human intervention.

At considerably lower cost and with significantly greater engagement of their natural settings, Fazio has also fashioned several other courses that acknowledge and integrate their desert surroundings. Two that stand out are the Estancia Club in Scottsdale, Arizona and the Quarry Course at La Quinta in the Coachella Valley of southern California. Each provide breathtaking views of mountain ranges—the former sits at the base of Pinnacle Peak Mountain, the latter in the high desert overlooking Palm Springs Valley beneath the Santa Rosa Mountains— and fully incorporate the desert terrain and ecology throughout their design. Like the Monument Course at Troon North in Scottsdale, a Tom Weiskopf and Jay Morrish design; Jack Nicklaus's Desert Highlands, also in Scottsdale; and the Mountain Course of La Quinta, fashioned by Pete Dye, both Estancia and the Quarry emphasize and embrace the boulders, cacti, and the natural topography of the surrounding desert and mountains. These are all courses that "leap the fence" and connect the garden and the wild. They demonstrate the rich palette that the desert provides for the game's pursuit as dramatic, challenging, and beautiful as any golfing setting.

14

Lost Links

Rumors of fairways,
all that's left of summer rounds—
and faithful foursomes

F OR THE TENTH consecutive year, the National Golf Foundation of the United States reported that many more golf courses closed in 2015 than opened: 203 golf facilities, 177 of which were 18-hole layouts, closed permanently in 2015, while only 17 such courses opened. This 10:1 ratio has remained fairly constant since 2006, when new golf course construction peaked after a 15-year run that saw more than 4,500 courses open throughout the country. The new courses largely accommodated an upwardly mobile golfing population that both looked to residential golfing communities for investment and lifestyle choices and who sought high-end golfing destinations for their vacations and getaways. Those golfing appetites fueled a 40 percent growth in the number of American courses over the previous two decades, but the onset of the global recession in 2007 effected a significant reduction in home sales necessary to support golf-oriented residential communities and curbed discretionary spending for other golf-related activities. The adverse impact on the pursuit of the game was the greatest since the years of the Great Depression and World War II.

Other factors have also contributed to the decline in the number of golf courses. These include the high costs of rounds and equipment, the discouraging length of time it takes to play a round or to develop a satisfactory level of proficiency in the game, high property tax rates, and strict environmental codes impacting golf course profit margins and cost containment measures taken at courses, such as less maintenance and weaker customer service, that drive players away in search of better value for their recreational dollars.

But the story is not all bleak, as there are powerful forces at work that, if properly understood and considered, can favorably impact the long-term prospects for the game and its venues of play. Foremost among these are the importance of a *sense of place* and the *power of choice.*

The former underscores that we are still at the beginning of a digital technology revolution that is remaking the economic and social geography of communities worldwide. These technological developments are, in fact, influencing a "placeless society." In other words, the digital revolution has provided unprecedented freedom to serve isolation and to do things alone.

Yet paradoxically, a sense of place has been gaining favor as a highly valued and desirable goal. As so many folks who fled cities and their crowded work environments in the 1970s and 1980s for a home in the suburbs or the appeal of gated golf communities have since discovered, there is something critically missing when flight and privacy take precedence over community and connection.

The *power of choice* recognizes that companies and individuals, also enabled by the digital revolution, can now locate more often where they *choose* and where they *will*, not just where they *must*, in order for the former to find a skilled workforce and the latter employment. The question of where to live has become increasingly contingent upon the character, attributes, and attractions of a location beyond such traditional business location factors as land costs, taxes, and the local and state regulatory environment.

Choosing where to live also acknowledges the relationship between a place and an individual's economic future and personal happiness. The message to towns and communities of various sizes and sorts—including golf communities—is the importance of a clear sense of identity, spirit, and values in order to attract and keep people who want not only to be a part of such a community but also to contribute to its well-being.

What these two factors enable is a "new localism," a renewed appreciation for the importance of place, where people can experience the arts, cultural amenities, entertainment, recreation, face-to-face meetings in real pubs and restaurants, and a "Main Street" *agora*, where shopping, business, local politics, and social encounters meet and mix naturally. These are places where the innate energy and creative joy of people define the scene, places where the quality of life is tangible and attractive to visitors and permanent residents alike. In short, *place matters*. And the golf club or community or course that recognizes this is as attuned to contemporary social trends as it is invested in its own success.

When these conditions exist along with a fair, challenging, and well-maintained and managed course, the prospects for a club's long term viability increase greatly. Not all, of course, will be able to resist the lucrative offers of residential and commercial real estate developers or withstand the eminent domain pressures for roadway construction and other public projects. Those forces doomed such wonderful early twentieth-century American designs as the Westhampton Country Club, Westhampton, New York (Charles Banks, architect); Mill Road Farm Country Club, Lake Forest, Illinois (William Flynn); Deepdale Golf Club, Great Neck, New York (Charles Blair Macdonald); Bayside Links, Bayside, New York (Alister Mackenzie); and Beaver Tail Golf Club, Jamestown, Rhode Island (A. W. Tillinghast). But those clubs and players and communities that recognize that an abandoned golf course hurts the local socioeconomic structure and causes more than just ecological change to the area—and who resolve not to let that happen to them—will be the ones with the best chance to turn the tide of course attrition and ensure the game's future expansion.

15

Home

Just to weigh the word,
home, and all that it summons—
how sweet its embrace.

MOST GOLFERS PLAY the majority of their rounds on one course. Whether that is a public or private course, the United States Golf Association reports that golfers posting handicaps indicate that almost 75 percent of their rounds are recorded at "home." This pattern of play is one of the reasons why golf instruction generally focuses on improving performance on a golfer's home course.

Understanding the demands of a home course and mastering the shots it requires are keys to gaining a "home course advantage" when competing against players who do not have such familiarity. But *home* is not just a venue where a game is played. It is also a place with emotional attachments. When these two dimensions are combined, the notion of home takes on deeper significance that can contribute greatly to the enjoyment of the game and appreciation for its fields of play.

Course familiarity embraces so much more than the shapes and yardages of holes, the speed and contours of greens, or the placement of bunkers and other hazards. If that was the extent of what knowing a course required, there would be little, if any, edge for the player who calls that course home. The real advantage comes from the *experience* of playing a course and understanding its quirks and mannerisms that course guides and descriptions cannot adequately convey. Like the homeowner who knows which floorboards creak in damp weather or where the puddles form in the backyard after a rain, the player who *lives* his home course is the one most likely to gauge its moods and to translate that understanding into good play.

This kind of familiarity also allows a player to anticipate the conditions of the course as it is affected by various factors. What are the consequences of the last night's rainstorm on the creek on the fifth? How has the summer drought affected the roll off the slope on the fourteenth? What influence does a change in the prevailing wind direction have throughout the course? To be sure, this insider knowledge flows from keen observation. But something more. It also reflects genuine appreciation, and indeed affection for the home grounds. It is to *know* more deeply this object of value and pleasure, and it is to *care* about it.

The delight in knowing the history, features, and idiosyncrasies of a player's home course certainly manifests itself in the way a player acknowledges such matters on his or her regular rounds. But it also provides great satisfaction—and pride—to the player who can pass along these tips and features to playing companions who lack that context or familiarity.

Yet there are times when too much information can get in the way of enjoying a round, when blissful ignorance might be the best guide to playing an unfamiliar course. There may be no course in the world where this is truer than the Old Course at St. Andrews. It is impossible to convey fully to a first-time player the eloquence, appeal, and treachery of golfing grounds that look so ordinary upon first glance nor to explain how the pure rudeness of the land and the circumstances of wind and sea constantly affect and shape it. It is perhaps better to just hit away rather than to contemplate all that awaits to be encountered and negotiated on these grounds. Course management can come later— although the moguls and mounds, burn and wall, bunkers and broom ensure that the marriage between strategy and serendipity will always be a bit rocky here.

Home also underscores how every course ends—a home hole. The final hole, often named "Home" or *Hame* on many Scottish courses, announces what on some days may be a thankful conclusion to a round that has not gone particularly well. Or more positively, it affords a final opportunity to appreciate the day, the course, and the company.

The world of golf has an extraordinary array of wonderful eighteenth holes: Pebble Beach, Harbour Town, Carnoustie, Adare, Royal Birkdale, Bay Hill, Doral (Blue), Winged Foot, Merion, Pine Valley, the Old Course at St. Andrews, TPC-Sawgrass, Riviera. The best combine setting, memorability, shot value, a summary of the character of the course, and excitement for players of all abilities. Yet no matter what a player's skill and familiarity with the course might be, the eighteenth hole signals that the journey of the round nears completion and a warm place of reverie and remembrance awaits—the home hearth of the nineteenth hole.

16

Nineteenth

Where the stories start,
days recounted and honored,
rounds both praised—and raised

T HERE IS A lovely scene in Michael Murphy's novel *Golf in the Kingdom* where he and his companions have just completed their round and are sitting before the blazing logs in the hearth of the clubhouse bar. With whisky glasses in hand, they are listening to members of the club singing Scottish golfing songs. It is the beginning of a long evening for Murphy. It would take him to the home of one of his playing partners for dinner and then back out to the course after midnight in search of a mysterious hermit who lived in a cave within the ravine bordering one of the holes. It is an evening spent "singing the praises of golf."[12]

It is an episode that celebrates one of the most distinctive rituals of the game. For the post-round camaraderie among the day's playing partners, competitors, and, for that matter, anyone else on the course that day underscores the social appeal of the game and reinforces the joy in sharing a common passion.

But more. Such gatherings connect to the history and the nature of the game, and the best nineteenth holes facilitate all of this. For there in the spike marks on wooden floors, the framed scorecards and photos of champions on the walls, views beyond the bar to the course just played, and drams of the Macallan and pints of Guinness are something more than atmosphere and refreshment. For here is a celebration of the spirit of the game, and for many golfers, no matter their score that day, the nineteenth is their favorite "hole" on the course.

Not every nineteenth hole, of course, has all of these elements, but there are places that are extraordinary exemplars of what the best golf bars and pubs have to offer—places like the Tap Room in the Lodge at Pebble Beach and the lounge/bar in the Dunvegan Hotel in St. Andrews. Neither provide a view of the famous courses they complement, but amid the impressive selection of single malts and ales are enough photos and memorabilia to rival the finest golf museums. And if only these walls could talk . . .

If it's views patrons seek, there are none better than those provided in the Sunset Grill at Arcadia Bluffs overlooking Lake Michigan or the Ryder Cup Bar of Kiawah's Ocean Course perched above the coastal lowland or both the STICKS bar and outdoor patio of Spanish Bay overlooking Monterey Bay. Spanish Bay even comes with a bagpiper who, like his counterparts at Arcadia Bluffs and a few other American courses, pipes a conclusion to each day's play.

All these places are appointed in tartan and wood and homage to both the local and grander history of the game. Particularly heavy on the local flavor are the Ryder Cup Lounge off the lobby of the Carolina Hotel at Pinehurst, which honors the 1951 Ryder Cup matches there and Donald Ross; the Tap Room in the Hollins House at Pasatiempo, which celebrates the collaborative genius of Alister Mackenzie and Marion Hollins; and Phil's Grill at the Grayhawk Golf Club in Scottsdale, Arizona, which is half bar and half shrine to Phil Mickelson.

There may be no warmer reception for visiting golfers after their rounds, though, than that provided by so many clubs in Ireland and Scotland. The lounges at Nairn, North Berwick, Waterville, Rosapenna, and

Royal Dornoch, for example, offer simple fare and an invitation "to sing the praises" with the local membership. As well as to join the good-spirited wagering focused on the performance of players finishing their rounds within their view.

Although the most cherished nineteenth hole may be at a player's home course, any place that helps golfers appreciate why they play and love this game is worthy of praise. For they offer a gentle reminder of the timeless reach of the game and its embrace. It is there within the old Scottish golfing saying: "The game was invented a billion years ago—don't you remember?" And it is there amid the toasts raised, the bets settled, and the memories made at the nineteenth hole.

17

Taste

Rich, fresh snapper soup,
with a dash of cream sherry—
tasting Pine Valley.

F OOD IS AMONG the most powerful agents we have to spark our
memories. Whether we recall a full meal or a single taste, food not
only can transport us to a particular time and place, but it can also
trigger deep feelings and emotions. Indeed, what we remember has as
much to do with the state of our mind and body in the present as it was
on the occasion of a memorable food experience.

There is, in fact, a physiological dimension to such memories because a
part of our brain called the hippocampus plays a vital role in enabling

us to recall very concrete images and narratives. This amazing zone has strong connections to other regions of the brain that channel our emotional memories and sense of smell. This helps explain why a certain smell might presage a vivid memory even before we consciously reconstruct the event, and of course, the more memorable the event, the more intense the association of food connected with that event.

The snapper soup at Pine Valley is not just a reward for completing a round on a course that has frequently been ranked the best in the world. It is a reminder that the experience of playing a place like Pine Valley transcends the course itself and includes all matter of ambience, aura, and anticipation. This dark, chunky bowl of soup—it is snapper the turtle, by the way, not red snapper the fish—is a local specialty in the Philadelphia area, and it does have its rivals, as, for example, a similar item on the menu at Merion. But the exclusive setting of Pine Valley, residing in its own municipal borough, lends a sense of unique privilege and timelessness to the entire scene. And the soup fits this bill perfectly, as various recipes for its making date to the eighteenth century in the United States.

Pine Valley is not unique, though, in enhancing a memorable golfing experience through food and drink. Pimento sandwiches at Augusta National, the burger dog at San Francisco's Olympic Club, onion soup at the Pebble Beach Tap Room, a pint of Belhaven at the Dunvegan bar just around the corner from the eighteenth green of the Old Course at St. Andrews, a Guinness after a round anywhere in Ireland, a dram of the McCallan in the Cabot Bar overlooking the seascape of Cape Breton, Nova Scotia, a local Oregon ale in McKee's Pub at Bandon Dunes—these are delicious affirmations that there is more to taste than the salty air of the links land, more to sniff than sweet pine and eucalyptus in pursuit of this game. It is a game for all seasons—and senses.

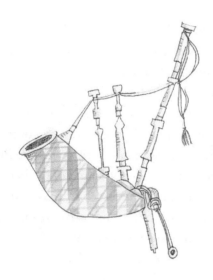

18

Pipes

In the harmony
between the chanter and drone
deep emotions rise

IS THERE A golfer whose soul cannot be stirred, whose memories of the game cannot be roused by the sounds of the Great Highland Bagpipe?

The skirl of the pipes that flows from the interplay between the melodies of the chanter and the steady hum of the drone compels attention and summons images of the game and its national home whenever it is heard. There may be no musical instrument so closely connected to a geographic region than the pipes and the Highlands of Scotland. Even Chaucer recognized the effect of the wails and cries that emanated from this instrument with a reference to it in *The Canterbury Tales*.[13]

The earliest verifiable evidence of the Highland pipes as an instrument of national identity flows from a French historical account of the Battle of Pinkie Cleugh in 1547. This engagement took place on the banks of the River Esk near the coastal town of Musselburgh in East Lothian. It did not go well for the earls of Scotland who opposed the efforts of Henry VIII to strengthen the English crown's control over their land and to replace Catholic religious authority with the Protestant Church of England. Neither unnerved by the sound of the bagpipes nor deterred by the numerical advantage of the forces arrayed against him, the Duke of Somerset employed both cavalry and offshore gun boats to dominate the battlefield. The Scots were routed in this last great pitched battle between the armies of Scotland and England. Two hundred years later, heralded again into battle by bagpipes, the Scots suffered a similar defeat at Culloden in 1746. This marked the last military uprising of the Highland clans against the English.

Yet the value of the pipes to announce, rally, and deploy military forces could not be denied, and their use was eventually appropriated by the British army. But the spirit of the pipes flowed from Scotland. When the pipes play, it is Scotland's voice. Just as surely, when golf is played, it is Scotland's game. The two are inextricably linked both as early elements of Scottish nationalism and as modern agents of the country's cultural influence.

The contemporary fascination with bagpipes has been driven by pageantry, commercialism, and curiosity, and it is rooted in the comfort and nostalgia they evoke. Whether in the grand setting of the assembled pipe and drum bands at Edinburgh Castle for the annual Edinburgh Military Tattoo or a summer evening parade of a Highland village's local corps, the pipes reach deep within memories and emotions. It is why they have increasingly played a part in weddings, funerals, military and civilian ceremonies, and other occasions.

For golfers, the sounds of a lone piper bringing the day's play to an end are particularly poignant. The effect can be chilling, spellbinding, and deeply personal. The sweet airs of "Amazing Grace" and "Auld Lang Syne" afford connection to everyone within their earshot. But so much more. The music of the pipes is another element of the culture of golf that invites listeners to ponder its hold and to savor its embrace.

19

Lost Ball

Searching for a ball
waiting to be discovered—
but by someone else

I have seen news videos of outfielders rummaging for
a baseball lost in the ivy on the quaintly leafy wall of
Wrigley Field, and I have experienced mishit tennis balls
flying over the court fence deep into an impenetrable
grove beyond; but no sport offers the sensation of lostness
as often and enragingly as does golf.

—John Updike[14]

"I'M NOT LOST," whispers the Nike golf ball with "TIGER" stamped on it, buried deep in the tall fescue rough off the first fairway of Royal St. Georges Golf Club. "I'm just hiding." Indeed it was, but it was not found by Tiger Woods or anyone else in his gallery and entourage in the five minutes they had to find his opening shot of the 2003 Open Championship. So back to the tee, Tiger marched with a two-stroke penalty for a lost ball. He finished the round with a 2-over par 73 and eventually lost the tournament by 2 shots to Ben Curtis, the 396th ranked player in the world at the time. The ball was eventually found by someone else who sold it at bid for a handsome price. Tiger was not its buyer.

Tiger was not alone in losing a ball in 2003. Just in the United States, the estimated number of golf balls lost or abandoned in a year is three hundred million. It may be closer to a half billion worldwide given that the American golfing population is about 60 percent of the world's total. The three hundred million lost balls in the U.S. average to about nine a golfer. That seems very conservative given the bad days that most golfers have had. The Ko'olau Golf Course on Oahu reports that in one round on one day, one player lost sixty-three balls to the dense rainforest that surrounds the entire course. That skews the average just a bit.

In ways both dramatic and ordinary, golf balls disappear. They find watery graves in the seas off Machrihanish and Old Head, in the lakes surrounding the island greens at Sawgrass and Coeur d'Alene, and in the marshlands of Harbour Town and Mission Bay. They are carried off by birds and dogs. They lodge into ancient rock walls at Tralee and North Berwick and standing cactus at Troon and Estancia. They disappear into pine forests, gorse bushes, grape vines, and azaleas, and they hide, almost in plain sight, under the fallen leaves of autumn and the brows of bunkers.

Yet millions of "lost" golf balls are retrieved each year. Over one hundred thousand balls *annually* are fished out of the lake surrounding the island green seventeenth at Sawgrass. They later reenter the game as "preowned" balls, which, it seems, is a kinder label for a lost ball than drowned and forsaken. In 2009, that same number of balls was discovered at the bottom of Loch Ness in Scotland by a submersible sonar device hunting for the loch's famous monster. Rather than blaming the monster, the balls were attributed to Scottish golfers around the loch's perimeter who had been using Nessie's pond as a driving range for years.

If losing a golf ball is a shared experience for golfers around the world, so is looking for a ball that may not be lost, just momentarily unfound. A curious blend of camaraderie, denial, and hope often accompanies the search. We've all been there before. Despite all evidence that the ball did indeed fly the boundary fence or sail over the cliff or splash into the creek, golfers will imagine an unseen ricochet off a tree or a rock or a miraculous skip across the water. After all, the rules allow a few minutes to look for the ball, and such good fortune has been rumored, perhaps even witnessed, for others.[15] The downcast return to the spot where the wayward shot was launched may be inevitable. But why despair too quickly? "Hope is the thing with feathers," wrote Emily Dickinson. A lovely reminder that golf balls were once a thing with feathers.

20

Bunkers

Odd shapes and old scrapes,
harmony and jeopardy
within the landscape

EVERY SAND BUNKER on every golf course in the world has a common ancestor. This was a patch of sand on a piece of links land that either some animal exposed while scraping out relief from the elements, or the wind and rain eroded while sweeping over those dunes and meadows. The relentless assault of the weather gradually enlarged those initial bare spots and burrows. Much later, as golf took hold on these lands, man-made areas of sand appeared from so many divots dug out of the ground where shots were frequently struck and they joined the naturally formed dips and depressions. And still later, as courses became more defined and architects brought more purposeful elements to the fields of play, these sandy pits and recessions were recognized as features that added character to the course and challenge to the game.

But it all started with a sheep in Scotland seeking shelter from a storm.

There are two main and not necessarily antithetical schools of thought among golf course designers about the purposes of bunkers, which were first identified by that name in the 1812 rules of golf. The harshest perspective emphasizes bunkers as a hazardous challenge that aims to punish a bad shot. The other, perhaps best expressed by Alister

Mackenzie, "is to make the game interesting."[16] That is, these are elements of a course that are *both* true obstacles *and* contributions to the challenge of the game and the aesthetics and enjoyability of its playing grounds.

This latter view also stresses that bunkers are more *strategically interesting* than other hazards, such as out-of-bounds or water areas, because the penalty for hitting into a bunker will vary with the recovery skills of the player. Bobby Jones recognized this distinction in a somewhat macabre explanation: "Getting in a water hazard is like being in a plane crash—the result is fatal. Landing in a bunker is similar to an automobile accident—there is a chance of recovery."[17]

Regardless of the ability of the player, though, there are some bunkers in the world of golf that are truly terrifying and capable of destroying both rounds and tournament hopes. Japan's Tommy Nakajima came to the par 4, seventeenth hole of the Old Course tied for the lead in the third round of the 1978 Open. He safely hit the difficult green with his second shot, coming to rest in the front right corner. The hole was cut back left, leaving him a forty-foot putt that needed to stay right of a ridge which bisected the green and sloped left toward a deep, greenside bunker—the infamous Road bunker. He was not successful. The ball caught the wrong side of the ridge and trickled down into the bunker. Four shots from the bunker later, he finally regained the putting surface. Two putts followed for a quintuple bogey nine. Nakajima went from tied for the lead to an eventual finish of seventeenth. And he left a new nickname in the bunker—the Sands of Nakajima.

Road is just one of the Old Course's 112 bunkers that are, perhaps, the course's greatest defense. They have bedeviled the game's best since the nineteenth century. After four failed attempts to extricate himself from Hill bunker on the par 3 eleventh, Bobby Jones walked off the course in frustration and out of the 1921 Open. And Hill is not even regarded as that hole's hardest bunker. This is a distinction generally conceded to the Strath pot bunker that sits against the face of the plateaued putting surface.

PAUL ZINGG

Jack Nicklaus descended into Hell—that is, the massive, ten-foot-deep, one-thousand-square-foot bunker on the par 5, fourteenth hole—in the opening round of the 1995 Open. Like Nakajima, it took Jack four shots to escape on his way to a quintuple bogey. Asked by a reporter who was not aware of the details of his play on fourteen how he managed a ten, Jack explained that he "missed a four-footer for a nine."

There are similarly nightmarish tales and harrowing memories in the deep, narrow "Coffin" on the 123-yard eighth hole at Royal Troon; the 40- foot deep "Himalayas" on the monstrous, 225-yard, par 3 fourth at Royal St. Georges; the furrows of the 100-yard long "Church Pews" between the third and fourth fairways at Oakmont; the insulting pot bunker planted in the middle of the green of the sixth at Riviera; hell again—this time, the vast sandy wastes of Hell's Half Acre—on the seventh at Pine Valley; and one of the oldest and largest bunkers in the game, the cavernous sand hazard awaiting players who surmount the dunes of the Alps, the seventeenth at Prestwick.

These storied venues, of course, are not the only places where great bunkering can be found. Often such places are right under a player's nose, if they know for what they are looking. Bunkers that combine challenge for the player and character for the course and offer strategic choices and aesthetic pleasures may be as close as a player's home course or the local muni. Wherever they may be, the key to their appreciation and encounter is as much the skill that is brought to the task of either avoiding or escaping them, as it is the mind-set that governs the effort. As Sam Snead said, "Of all the hazards, fear is the worst." Yet with a healthy attitude and smart play, one can handle any hazard, even hell—Hell bunker, that is.

21

Remembering

Shadows on the tee,
our companions for the round,
and friends whom we've lost

T HE IMPORTANCE OF memory in golf is one of the game's most
compelling elements. It is engrained in the broad social fabric of
the game through the history and culture of the sport, and it plays out
in uniquely personal ways through the nature of the game. Both the
communal and individual aspects of the game are present every time a
round is played.

Like every sport, golf has a history that is tied to specific locations
and events; but like no other sport, golf sustains the memory of its
great and dramatic moments by providing unique access to the places
of their occurrence. Unlike, for example, a seat in the Rose Bowl or
courtside at Wimbledon or a field box at Yankee Stadium, golf permits
its fans and players a literal feel for the scene and the action. This
personalized experience entails more than close inspection of famous
acres while strolling across them as a tournament spectator. On public
access courses such as the Old Course at St. Andrews or Pebble Beach,
it includes the opportunity not only to play historic grounds but also
to experience shots from the exact locations where history was made.

Consider two examples involving Tom Watson on these very courses. Battling Seve Ballesteros in the final round of the 1984 Open at the Old Course, Watson hit his second shot on the par 4 seventeenth too far, and it came to rest within three feet of the stone wall that borders the road adjacent to the green. From there, he could manage no better than a bogey, dropping him two behind Ballesteros with one hole to play. Two years earlier, in the final round of the 1982 U.S. Open at Pebble Beach, Watson had faced a similar situation. This time, he was going head-to-head with Jack Nicklaus in the final round. And this time, it was not an ancient wall but fierce greenside rough also on the seventeenth hole, which challenged him. Yet on that occasion, he played one of the greatest shots in U.S. Open history, popping the ball out of the rough and into the cup for a birdie that sealed his victory.

For anyone playing the Old Course or Pebble Beach, especially on the latter when the flagstick is set back left in the traditional final round Open location, attempting shots from those spots on those holes has become something of a ritual. Yet it is not just history that is invoked. It is also a player's skill that is engaged. And this underscores just how *personal* memory is in the execution of one's play.

Throughout a golfer's history with the game, there are countless swings stored in his or her memory. Whether these are memories about courses or rounds or specific shots, they can be both good and bad. The issue is not if memories exist, but which are recalled—and which can be trusted. How well can we recall the memory of a shot successfully executed in a similar situation? How effectively can we exorcise the demons of a failed shot or the distractions of places on a hole where we do *not* want the ball to go? How readily can we summon the good memories that our brains have planted in our muscles in order to make a solid hit?

The personal and the social especially converge when we play a round with old friends. For on such occasions, especially if there has been a lengthy time between them, there is a chance not only to forge new memories but also to reaffirm the pleasure of company who have made the game meaningful and enjoyable to us for so many years.

To be sure, *all* memories are a part of us, even, of course, those that recall pain and disappointment. The issue is not to deny them. The double bogey on the eighteenth that cost a match did, in fact, happen. Rather, it is to avoid dwelling on such thoughts so that they inform our future but do not determine it.

More importantly and positively, memory allows us to hold on to what we value and love. And in those long stretches of time, when, for whatever reason, we are absent from playing golf, memory is a gift that keeps the game and the reasons why we play it—and with whom—clear and close. It is to appreciate the words of James Matthew Barrie, the Scottish writer who introduced the world to Peter Pan, that a reason why we have memory is "that we may have roses in December." Roses and birdies and treasured companions, no matter how distant.

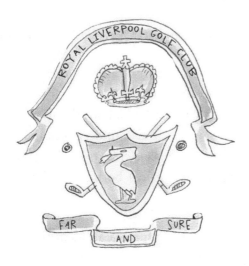

22

Far and Sure

Here where the round starts,
facing the grounds and the day,
the sound of honor

THERE IS A lovely scene early in *Tommy's Honour*, the well-received 2016 film about the relationship between Old Tom Morris and his son, Tommy, and their impact on the modern game of golf that says as much about them as the game itself.[18] As young Tom begins to show promise in the game, he is encouraged by his father to join him for rounds on the course of St. Andrews, where Old Tom is the custodian of the links. These rounds anticipated the times when they would become a formidable team together in foursome money matches against players from other clubs in the area. In this scene, Tommy is fifteen years old.

As they approach the first tee, Tommy says to his father "Far and sure, Da."

To which, Old Tom nods and gently replies, "Far and sure."

It is a sweet moment that reflects the warmth and earnestness that director Jason Connery aimed to achieve in his film. In this fashion, the brief exchange is a subtle revelation of both the affection and the rivalry between father and son. Yet it also underscores the invitation within a round of golf to engage those elements of the game—distance and accuracy—wherein success against both par and an opponent largely depend.

The annals of golf are not very precise in identifying when the phrase "far and sure" entered the lexicon of the game, but a key moment that affirmed its use occurred in the aftermath of a famous match on the Leith links in 1681 pitting the Duke of York (the future King James II of England) and a local player and ballmaker, John Patersone, against two English noblemen. The latter had challenged the duke with the notion that golf was an "English" game, and the match would settle their claim. The duke and his partner won the world's first "international" match handily and earned bragging rights for Scotland.

With his share of the sizeable purse, Patersone bought a house in the Canongate district of old Edinburgh. He named the place "Golfer's Land." The duke authorized Patersone to attach a stone escutcheon richly detailed with heraldic symbols, including a hand grasping a golf club, to the front of the six-story stone building. Inscribed across the top of the shield were the words "far and sure." It seems likely that Patersone chose a phrase that would be recognizable to golfers and others who passed by his house. Although heraldry is coded, it is not abstruse. A recognizable golfer's saying seemed most appropriate for a golfer's house in a golfer's land.

Since the seventeenth century, "far and sure" has been adopted by many clubs and golfing societies to proclaim and honor their approach to the game. The Royal Burgess Golfing Society of Edinburgh, for example, actually changed its motto from "Long and Far" to Patersone's more encompassing and textured phrase soon after the organization became a legal corporation in the early nineteenth century. Both the Royal Liverpool Golf Club in England and the Chicago Golf Club in the United States, founded, respectively, in 1869 and 1895, inscribed "Far and Sure" on their club crests. The many championships conducted at both courses—among them twelve Opens at the former, and three U.S. Opens, four U.S. Amateurs, and two Walker Cups at the latter— attest to the demands of courses that proclaim distance, accuracy, and steadfastness as hallmarks of their nature.

"'Far and sure! Far and sure!' 'Twas the cry of our fathers,'" begins Sheriff Logan's nineteenth-century drinking song about golf.[19] But more than just a call to brothers in the game to drain a few pints, it proclaims that "there is honour and hope in the sound." For director Jason Connery and screen writer Kevin Cook to have inserted this phrase into the film *Tommy's Honor* was not only to capture the spirit of the nineteenth-century game but also to appreciate Old Tom's subsequent dedication to honor his son's memory after his tragic death at age twenty-four. For as the song implores, let "Far and Sure" "guide us in Golf . . . [and] let it guide us in life."

23

Tools

Boughs of beech and birch,
supple and strong in the wind—
and for the Scot's game

GREAT STANDS OF beech, ash, hickory, and hazel have long filled the forests of North America and Western Europe. They were familiar to those ancient shepherds who fashioned their crooks from these hard woods and then decided to propel a rock across the grazing rounds of their sheep toward a target.

The supple yet strong quality of these woods (and others such as yew and elm) shaped many an English longbow too. Throughout the Hundred Years' War of the fourteenth and fifteenth centuries between the English and the French, the longbow was a fearsome weapon that decided many battles, most notably Crecy (1346) and Agincourt (1415). But tactics and other weapons, especially firearms, eventually neutralized the longbow, and it returned to its original use as a tool for hunting and sport. But for centuries, the longbow allowed a man to launch an object farther than any other self-propelled means. A sturdy archer could fly an arrow nearly four hundred yards.

It was not surprising then that the first golfers who sought clubs other than the crude instruments, which they might fashion themselves, turned to bow-makers for their manufacture. What they sought were clubs with the same properties as the best longbows—durable instruments that provided, first and foremost, distance.

It also seems to be the case that some early golfers were willing to pay a high price for an equipment edge over their competitors. Imagine that. Even at the dawn of the game, the siren song of greater distance was irresistible. King James IV of Scotland heard it in 1502, when he purchased a full set of clubs from a bow-maker in Perth, who may have been the first club maker to advertise his clubs through the player who used them. Royal woods, after all, does have a nice ring to it.

The king's clubs were all-wooden instruments, as would be the norm for golfers until well into the nineteenth century. This is mainly because the ball that was used—a goose feather-stuffed, leather-stitched, rounded object about the same size as the modern ball—was vulnerable to cracks and abrasions when struck by metal "irons" or the bone inserts in wooden club faces. The "featheries" were also quite expensive, so it was important to keep them in play for as long as possible. Different woods advanced the playing capabilities of clubs, though, especially the use of American hickory for shafts and the gradual preference for another American hardwood, persimmon, for club heads.

Over the course of the next century, club design generally followed improvements in the ball. The "guttie," a solid ball molded from dried gum resin, made golf balls both more affordable and durable, although they traveled about the same distance as a featherie. But the surface of the guttie allowed for some manipulation, and soon, ballmakers were marking the surface with various cuts and patterns to effect both distance and ball control. The harder surface of the guttie also meant that they were more tolerant of hits from clubs forged in iron. The era of a set of clubs made entirely of wood was over.

The most dramatic leap forward in ball design came with the award of a patent to American businessman and inventor Coburn Haskell in 1899 for a rubber core and wound ball within a gutta-percha cover. In an instant, the "Haskell" ball transformed the game. It flew farther, lasted longer, and proved more maneuverable than any ball before it. Bobby Jones considered the Haskell as the first "modern" ball and the most significant development in the history of golf.

The new ball inspired great experimentation with club design. Steel replaced hickory for shafts and then was challenged by graphite. Stainless-steel replaced persimmon for "wood" heads and then bowed to titanium. Chemistry, applied physics, and computer-assisted design replaced wood-curing, leather-tanning, and boxes of nails in the clubmaker's workshop.

No doubt King James, the Gentlemen Golfers of Edinburgh, Old Tom Morris, Harry Vardon, and even Bobby Jones would be hard-pressed to recognize what their game has wrought in terms of the tools to play it. Variable thickness soles, perimeter-weighted and cavity-backed irons, rolled cup face technology, instantaneous adjustment loft and face angle settings, MOI design, "fitting science," tungsten weighting, triaxial carbon crowns. But they would recognize what these clubs promise—faster ball speed, more forgiveness, greater accuracy, and longer distance.

In their day, the importance of swing principles, playing experience, passion, and practice were the keys to achieving these goals; and even in the post-modern world of the fourth industrial revolution, these matters still count.[20] For regardless of the tools in a golfer's hand or the ball that is played, these factors underscore the essential timelessness of the game and its human dimensions. No matter what the new clubs promise, they cannot change the nature of a game that combines skill, chance, whimsy, and luck so seamlessly and fully. The secret to success in the game, as Hogan said, is still "in the dirt" and between the ears. Although there is no denying the satisfaction that comes from pounding a drive even farther than a medieval longbowman could launch an arrow.[21]

24

Divine Presence

To feel the divine
gaze upon the timeless grounds—
and join the game there

T HE BIG NAME Pro stands on a high point overlooking a grand
landscape. What he surveys could be a wooded mountain valley,
a seaside sweep of dunes, rolling foothill country, or the high desert.
It makes no difference. Like the explorers depicted in the murals of so
many American public buildings in the 1930s that commemorated the
nation's westward course of empire, he gazes heroically, knowingly, at
the scene before him. One hand holds a map of the area he overlooks.
The other points vaguely to a spot in the distance. A convenient
photographer captures the exact moment when the Big Name Pro
proclaims: "I've never seen such a spectacular setting. Surely, God
intended that a golf course be built here."

A slight variation of the Big Name Pro is the World Famous Architect.
Sometimes they are the same, but regardless, this is a familiar moment
in golf course construction around the world, even as some sites might
raise an eyebrow about the infinite wisdom of God to imagine a course
there. It is not necessarily obvious, for example, that God intended
a golf course to be built on landfills and marshlands, in abandoned
rock quarries, and jungles. There may be no land in the world of golf,

though, with fewer doubts about the hand of God in anything about the game than Ireland.

Perhaps, most fundamentally, this is because Ireland is a land of deep spiritual memory and presence. From the Neolithic deities who abided in the land when Ireland was first inhabited to the one Christian God and registry of saints who have been invoked by both Catholics and Protestants through civil wars and "Troubles," Ireland has been haunted and defined by spiritual influence, especially affecting the relationship of its people to the land. This has been a constant element of Irish history and culture. It has formed a strong thread that has run clearly through Ireland's connected "worlds"—Celtic and English, Catholic and Protestant, planter and Gael, loyalist and nationalist, agrarian and urban, civilian and barbarian, Christian and pagan, immigrant and emigrant, ancient and modern, mythic and true.

In short, Ireland is "an idea with many histories" and a place where the sacred and the supernatural are everywhere in the Irish experience, both on the surface and beneath.[22]

Including the country's golf courses.

Arnold Palmer encountered this spirit among the western cliffs and coastline of Tralee, where he found land "ideally suited for the building of a golf course." What he fashioned in the dunes above the broad Banna Strand is a course that proclaims: "Created by God, Designed by Arnold Palmer."

At age seventy-four, Robert Trent Jones Sr. was invited to lay out a new course among the mountainous dunes adjacent to the Old Course at Ballybunion. "I was given a once-in-a-lifetime opportunity," he said about the Cashen Course, which opened in 1984. "The property I had to work with is perhaps the finest piece of links land in the world . . . an outrageously beautiful stretch of God-given land."

Joe Carr, Ireland's greatest amateur champion, was part of the design team that planted a golf course on top of the Old Head peninsula on the southern coast of County Cork. His work moved one reviewer to conclude that "If God were going to play golf, He would definitely pick the Old Head of Kinsale as His home course."[23]

But God may have already chosen his course. With a designer pedigree of Old Tom Morris, Harry Vardon, and Harry S. Colt and blessed with extraordinary views of heather-strewn hills, distant mountains, and village steeples, Royal County Down is "the kind of golf that people play only in their dreams," wrote the great golf writer Bernard Darwin. Against the magnificent backdrop of the Mountains of Moure and along the golden sands of Dundrum Bay, it is "the links of heaven."[24]

These four hardly exhaust the list of courses in Ireland where the intentions of Providence have been pondered. Indeed, it is not just heavenly grace that is praised here. It is heavenly assistance that is summoned to face their challenges. For just as Ireland has been blessed, vexed, and visited by the gods for eons, so too its golf courses afford all manner of charm and celebration, torment and temptation. The game in this land is an experience no golfer should miss.

PEOPLE AND PLACE

25

The Master

Arnie's Army,
hanging on hope—
Augusta in April.

WHEN ARNOLD PALMER stood on the first tee of the Augusta National Golf Club on Thursday, April 8, 2004, spectators pressed five-deep against the ropes around the tee box. This would continue throughout his round, the gallery numbers and cheers growing steadily, reaching their apex on the eighteenth green as he completed a round of 84. He missed the cut for the weekend by twenty shots, and no one, except perhaps, Arnie, was upset.

This was Palmer's record fiftieth consecutive Masters appearance—and his last as a player. Although he had not made the cut since 1983, when he tied for thirty-sixth, he had not had a top 10 finish since 1967, when a five-under performance in the weekend rounds vaulted him to fourth place. That fourth place finish put the cap on an extraordinary run between 1957 and 1967, when Palmer won the Masters four times, finished in the top 5 another five times, and never finished worse than ninth.

These were the years that laid the foundation for Palmer's career and mystique. In so doing, they witnessed the transformation of the Masters from an elite, clubby gathering barely glimpsed through grainy black-and-white television images to a global phenomenon that officially launched the golfing year and the annual quest for immortality that a win in a Major represented. Palmer and his two greatest rivals at Augusta, Jack Nicklaus and Gary Player, won eight of nine Masters during this stretch, and their exploits and personalities could not have been better scripted in Hollywood.

Or in Palmer's case, for a camera. Confident, charismatic, and arresting, he relished the game's unique set of physical and cerebral demands. And he endured its humbling realities. The Masters was his great stage for all of this. Final round charges to glory and all-too-human, heartbreaking missteps to defeat. And as much as Nicklaus and Player won the crowds with their heroics and class, none won the hearts of the Augusta patrons such as Palmer. And no player, not even six-time champion Nicklaus, had a stronger identification with the Masters than Palmer.

As the years went on and Palmer's skills diminished, the hopes of Arnie's Army for him went from winning the tournament to making the cut and to turning in a good round. But with no less enthusiasm. He knew that too and never missed an opportunity to reward his faithful followers with a thumbs-up, a look in the eye, and a memory.

26

Perfection

*The game prompts and tempts
with notions of perfection—
and nods to Hogan.*

BEN HOGAN WAS once asked if the score for a perfect round of golf would be eighteen under par. "No," replied Hogan, "a perfect round would be 18."

Even for someone whose peers on the professional golf tour said worked harder than anyone else, such a score was impossible. Even in his dreams. For Hogan once confessed to a dream in which he holed his tee shot on the first seventeen holes he played but lipped out on the eighteenth. But Hogan's response was neither arrogant nor ridiculous. It was honest. And if anything, honesty and the candor that accompanied it marked Hogan's manner and persona and contributed to his mystique.

Sometimes that honesty was harsh. As for example, when Nick Faldo, who won six Majors (three Opens and three Masters) among his forty professional tournament wins worldwide but never a United States Open, once asked Hogan how to win a U.S. Open. Hogan's answer was brusque, simple—and true—"Shoot the lowest score."

What these two anecdotes reveal about Hogan is that the essence of scoring transcends performance in any given round. To be sure, the scorecard tally reveals much about how the demands of par have been handled on a given day. But how one has prepared for a round, especially how one respects the spirit and honors the rules of the game, reflects not only the conduct of one's play but also the content of one's character.

On one level, a player will never know how accomplished he or she is in this game unless it is played within the rules. It may be tempting when playing a practice round to improve the lie of the ball a little or claim a mulligan when the first flies out of bounds or give oneself a few three-foot putts. Then what a shock it is to see scores leap by several strokes when playing strictly by the rules.

On another and more profound level, playing by the rules has everything to do with integrity. The game, of course, demands this. But so much more. As a player and as a person, it establishes reputation and measures trustworthiness. We will never be honest with others—we will never be trusted by others—if we are not honest with ourselves. And just as surely, we will never find our true place on the golfing ladder if we do not do so honestly. To bring honest effort and play to the game is to foster self-discovery and to find harmony with this game.

Hogan's notion of a perfect round recognized the obvious, as unattainable as it was, but it also revealed how contextual the quest for perfection is, that is, how dependent upon each player's skills and will the nature of the quest and its outcome can be. Hogan's obsession with achieving perfection in this least perfectible of games was shaped by *his* experience and *his* aspirations. It was *his* definition, and it created an aura of inapproachability and inscrutability about him. His abrupt and guarded manner permitted few close friendships and scant access to his world.

But his game was irresistible. Intimidated and fascinated, awestruck and reverent, his fellow professionals, fans, celebrities, and the media were drawn to him. Some came hoping to discover his much ballyhooed "secret" and left even more intrigued when he curiously said it was "in the dirt." Most came to watch the game's most dedicated craftsman at work. Few connected the dots. Few, that is, recognized that Hogan's quest for perfection focused on his ability to recall and trust the memory of a good swing; and that memory was formed "in the dirt," the countless hours of study and practice that gave him great pleasure and where he developed confidence in that what he recalled would be true. What surely frustrated Hogan and confounded those who watched him was his own admission that he rarely hit more than a half-dozen shots a round that performed exactly as he envisioned.

"He was our ideal," said four-time Open champion Peter Thompson, who finished runner-up to Hogan at Carnoustie in 1953. "He was the standard to which we all aspired, but none ever reached." Hogan's win at Carnoustie was the only time that he competed in the Open Championship, and his victory there enabled him to win all four of professional golf's modern Majors, something which only four other players have accomplished.

It is small consolation to know that Hogan often fell short of reaching his goals too, but he never stopped trying to "own his swing" and to find his place in the game. And perhaps, this is the most important lesson from the man known as "The Hawk" because of his fierce focus and iron will. For if reaching his plane of performance is not within our realm of possibility, appreciating his framework is.

27

Homage to Tom Watson

Let the seas pound,
let the rains pour—
another perfect day.

"WIND AND RAIN," said Tom Watson, "are great challenges. They separate the real golfers."

He should know.

A winner of seventy-one professional tournaments worldwide spanning five decades of play, his career tallies eight Major championships, ranking him sixth all-time among Major championship winners. His victories include five Open Championships, four achieved in Scotland. In 2009, at age fifty-nine, he nearly won a sixth claret cup there again at Turnberry. Leading the Open after the third round (making him the oldest player ever to lead a round in any Major), he bogeyed his seventy-second hole to fall into a tie with Stewart Cink, who subsequently defeated Watson in a four-hole playoff.

Watson's greatness can be attributed to many factors, but none more fully than his acceptance of the conditions of play at any time and place and his eagerness to embrace the challenges they represented. The unique circumstances of coastal links land and the often harsh weather that shaped, vexed, and visited these venues fit his temperament and spirit perfectly.

Serious weather for golfing, of course, is not an anomaly in Scotland. Yet second only to Scotland in the number of links land courses, Ireland will often experience even harsher conditions as great movements of air and ocean form in the Atlantic Ocean and fall upon the Emerald Isle, especially its western counties. Although a different ocean, the same is true for Pebble Beach, Spanish Bay, and Spyglass on the Monterey Peninsula in California, Chambers Bay along the shores of Puget Sound in the state of Washington, and a set of modern "classic" courses firmly established on top 100 lists that are congregated near the town of Bandon on the central coast of Oregon.

Roof-rattling wind and rain, the kind of weather that Nobel laureate Heinrich Boll described as "absolute, magnificent and frightening," effects the very nature of the game in places that experience it and compels both acceptance and adaptation if a player is to do more than merely survive a round. Weather, in fact, strengthens the bond between golf and the land on which it is played. For golf, like no other game, is as much shaped by the land as joined to it, and serious weather forces that connection. It necessitates that the game be played a lot closer to the ground than high above it in the howling breezes.

In short, with wind and rain, but absent firm but absorbent sandy soil, hearty seaside grasses, and topographic conditions that generally define links land golf, the game would be impossible there. It would also lack the aesthetic pleasure of the distinctive crunch that occurs when a well-struck iron compresses a ball upon the thin layer of fescue grass that covers the ground of these courses.

Watson embraced these elements of the total golfing experience, and yes, they took him to championships and glory but even more so to the inner joy and satisfaction that awaits any player who plays such courses and recognizes their connection to the very beginnings and nature of the game itself.

28

First Tee

Anticipation—
your home course or the Old Course,
it is all the same.

WHETHER IT IS with the regular weekend foursome on your home course or the ghosts of generations of golfers who have preceded you to "Burn" the opening hole of the Old Course at St. Andrews, it is impossible to ignore the nervous energy or deny the hopes for the day's round that accompany the walk to the first tee. No matter how familiar or foreign the setting, players bring both anticipation and excitement to this moment and the journey that is about to begin. With a little luck and commitment, that journey provides a memorable experience for all the right reasons.

Any journey worth the undertaking invites such a perspective, and to be sure, the notion of journey is one that is central to golf. On one hand, a round of eighteen holes covers a particular landscape. It is a physical expedition. On the other, the round offers the prospect of achieving both greater proficiency in the game and a stronger awareness of one's relationship with it. It is a means to self-discovery.

What transpires on the journey may not rival the trials of Odysseus, but it does evoke his epic of exile and return. For a round of golf, after all, is just that—*a round.* It circles us back to the clubhouse, the point of initial embarkation. It marks the conclusion of a player's engagement with the day's challenges and opportunities no matter how triumphant or miserable they may have been. On some days of particular struggle, the sight of the clubhouse beyond the eighteenth green is a welcome signal that the day's ordeal is over. On others, though, this sight has a bittersweet appeal. It is reward and regret, the end of the quest and the boundary of pleasure.

But all rounds begin with the first hole. For here, as the great golf architect Donald Ross noted, a "handshake" with the course takes place, and its qualities of landscape, setting, character, and design intent are first manifest.

Very few first holes among the world's thirty-three thousand courses convey all the qualities of the golfing experience that awaits as a round progresses. Many—Spyglass Hill, Bethpage Black, Ardglass, Oakmont, Doonbeg, Royal Lytham and St. Annes, Prestwick, Ko'olau, Augusta National, Bay Hill, Kapalua Plantation—come close, but in ways both restrained and dramatic, here are two that succeed in accomplishing the full introduction that Ross described.

Among the more subtle previews of what awaits is the first at Merion. Its cozy tee box sits only a few feet from a dining veranda, where, as Arnold Palmer once cautioned, you could tip over a tea cup with your club if you weren't careful. Measuring 362 yards from the back tees, the hole is only a few yards less than the average length of all the holes on the course. Twelve bunkers (a variety of fairway, crossing, and greenside) introduce players to Merion's 125 "white faces." A grove of tall pines in the corner of the right dogleg and a dense tree line along a roadside boundary to the left underscore the demands of accuracy and feelings of intimacy that define the entire course. The small, pear-shaped green, angled Redan-style away from the usual landing area off the tee, offers a variety of devilish cup placements. In his near-perfect 67 in the final round of the 1981 U.S. Open, David Graham sealed his victory by hitting every green and every fairway—except number 1.

For sheer drama, there is no more spectacular way to open a round than the first at Machrihanish. Laid out by Old Tom Morris in 1879 on the tip of the Kintyre Peninsula in southwest Scotland, the course follows the natural contours of the perfect links land that parallels the meeting of the Sound of Jura with the Irish Sea. "Battery" is a classic risk/reward hole. From an elevated tee, the hole requires a forced, dogleg left carry across a broad beach, tempting players to cut off as much as they dare on the 423-yard par 4. The hole hugs the beach the entire way, a point reinforced with a sign staked in the sand that warns walkers: "DANGER: First tee above. Please move farther along the beach." Yes, the beach is in play. An additional charm of the hole—besides its brave challenge and full exposure to the wind and rain that often sweeps across the peninsula—is its intimidating proximity to the golf shop and starter's area. A gallery is always there to watch and judge a player's first strike.

These are two very different holes in two very different settings, but they both effectively convey what a great opening hole can accomplish. They set the tone for a round and raise expectations for the journey ahead. It is a thrill on such holes to hear the starter say "Hit away!"

29

Fairways

Tee shot finds the rough,
"fairways are overrated"—
says the big hitter

B UT ARE THEY?
Besides scoring average, the three statistics that golfers rely upon most for an assessment of the state of their games are the numbers of putts, fairways hit, and greens in regulation over an 18-hole round. A Google search for the information that is available for golfers in the pursuit of improvement in these areas bears this out. By a 5 to 1 margin (517 million hits to 105 million), putting commands the internet. Driving ranks second followed by greens in regulation with 617,000 entries. The focus on driving favors those who want to hit the ball farther by about a 2 to 1 margin over those who seek greater accuracy off the tee.

Although there is little data that provides a statistical profile of amateur or "average" players, there is no shortage of data for the tour professionals. What it tells us regarding the debate between distance versus accuracy off the tee is actually well worth noting for the great majority of golfers whose average score significantly exceeds those elite few who make a living on the world's professional tours. According to the National Golf Foundation, the average score for an American male player is 97. That is a few less than the average of 100 for the same group about a decade ago, which suggests some positive effect on handicaps through technological advances for equipment and golf balls. But not much. And a major caveat: what the National Golf Foundation reports are average scores *only for players with established handicaps*, so it is very likely that the true average score for all male golfers is higher.

Lest the notion of a meaningful connection between the average player's score and that of Jordan Spieth produce only dismissals and fantasies, consider these data points from the PGA tour on fairway accuracy, greens in regulation, and score. Over the last five years, the tour *average* for hitting fairways has been about 63 percent. The tour *leaders* in this category can hit as high as 75 percent of their fairways. The tour average for players who hit greens *from the fairway* is about 65 percent. For players who hit greens *from the rough*, it is only 44 percent.

Even considering the superior ability of the pros to manage par (or better) when missing a green, they still lose an average of .16 strokes a hole every time they miss a green in regulation. In other words, the difference between hitting a green in regulation 65 percent of the time versus 44 percent over eighteen holes is almost two strokes a round.[25] That can be the difference between making the cut or not, between retaining one's tour card or not. It is a significant gap.

It is an even more significant figure for players who will hit considerably fewer fairways and greens in regulation than the pros. The player who regularly shoots in the mid-90s, for example, may hit only four or five fairways and only one or two greens in regulation in a typical round.

So what are the lessons here—besides working constantly on the short game? If the bottom line is to shoot lower scores, then the surest way to do that is to put yourself in the best position to achieve more pars per round. And the strongest common denominator for pros and amateurs alike that translates into lower scores is hitting more greens in regulation. Good ball striking, of course, will yield both distance and direction. But the evidence suggests that golfers—especially "average" players—are hurt more by inaccuracy off the tee than lack of distance.

Course and individual hole conditions such as light rough, open terrain, and large receptive greens may invite a more aggressive driving approach, and if the reason for whaling away is considered and strategic, why not? But pride does, in fact, go before the fall—or the bogey or worse. Remember, the most important distance to handle is not the three-hundred-yard drive to satisfy your ego and impress your friends but the five inches from ear to ear where in every shot finds its purpose and design.

30

Caddies

Humpin' the land,
totin' the bag,
workin' the tools

THEY ARE COMPANIONS and raconteurs, psychologists and savants. They are guides, sages, and allies who counsel, cajole, and even coerce.

They are twelve years old—and seventy-two. They are veteran philosophers of the links who spin tales of enlightenment and amusement, and they are gnarled rummies of the yards who reek of pints and cigarettes. They are schoolboys and schoolgirls who seek their loops during the summer months only, and they are tradesmen and women who follow the sun all year round.

At one end of their spectrum are the elite few who make more than a million dollars a year on the world's grandest stages, and at the other there are those who earn less than minimum wage on the fringes of the game.

Some have been with their "man" for decades. Most for just a few seasons. They have no job security. They can be dismissed in the middle of a season—or a round. The success of their player may occasionally merit his or her public praise, and occasionally, they will claim it themselves.

They are senior partners with their players, providing constant advice and service and leaving only the matter of hitting the ball to the player, and they are simple bag carriers who lug bags and try not to get in the player's way.

They are caddies, and they have been a part of the game for nearly four centuries.

Hidden in the veiled annals of the game are the origins of their appearance. Mary, Queen of Scots, whose enthusiasm for golf is only somewhat better documented, is often credited with employing caddies as club carriers for her games when she lived in exile in France from 1548 to 1561. The term may derive from the French *les cadets*, referring to young military school cadets. As often was the case, the Scots appropriated French terms for their own use, and the transition from *cadet* to *cawdy* (an eighteenth-century Scottish term referring to a porter) to caddy may have occurred quite naturally. Whatever its origins, caddy had become the familiar term for the man who "may carry the clubs, or run before the players," as duly noted in the Minutes of the Society of St. Andrews Golfers for June 27, 1771.

What is also certain is the transformation of the status of the caddy from a *tradesman* who merely carried clubs and spotted balls to a *craftsman* whose knowledge of the course and ability to "work the tools," that is, assess a player's strengths and weaknesses, including his attitude toward the game, contributed to his worth. For many of these caddies, often members of the clubs where they offered their services, this role was an extension of their familiarity with the game gained through proficiency as a player or some other aspect of the game. Andrew Dickson, for example, who lived near the Leith links in Edinburgh, was a ball maker who earned recognition as a caddy for the Duke of York, the future King James II of England, in a match in 1682. Old Tom Morris, Jamie Anderson, and Allan Robertson all started their golfing lives as caddies, and their subsequent success as players and architects was informed by what they observed "working the land" and carrying another's bag.

The modern company of professional caddies on the major world tours is an elite breed with little connection to their nineteenth-century predecessors beyond the basic task of carrying a bag and working as an independent contractor. The most famous among them are celebrities in their own right, linked synonymously with players in the prime of their careers: Mike "Fluff" Cowan with Peter Jacobson, Tiger Woods, and, later, Jim Furyk; Steve Williams with Woods, post-Fluff; Jim "Bones" Mackay, and Phil Mickelson; Tip Anderson and Arnold Palmer; Angelo Argea and Jack Nicklaus; Alfred "Rabbit" Dyer and Gary Player; Bruce Edwards and Tom Watson; Andy Martinez with Johnny Miller and Tom Lehman; Terry McNamara and Annika Sorenstam; Fanny Sunesson with Nick Faldo and Henrik Stenson; Herman Mitchell and Lee Trevino; Joe Lacava and Fred Couples; Ricci Roberts and Ernie Els. These are not the kind of folks who are waiting in the caddy shack for a weekend loop.

But those who are offer something upon which a price is impossible to put. This is memorability. For the best caddies welcome the responsibility of trust that a player places in him for the round ahead. They bring understanding of the features of the course to the first tee and an eagerness to translate that familiarity to the enjoyment of the round and the successful play of their "man," regardless of the qualities of the player's game. These baggers know their course well; they appreciate the effects of weather conditions and maintenance matters on it; and they anticipate how to negotiate all that awaits. But mainly, they are committed to providing a player with a memorable experience enhanced through the pleasure of their company. It is a perspective that aims to conclude a round with fond recollection—and, often a new friend. There may be no more important reason to praise—and to employ— the caddy.

31

Island

Safely bound it flies,
rudely drowned it dies—
Sawgrass seventeen.

I T HAS BEEN said that we really don't play the great holes—they
play us. Yes, they challenge us with their design, where they come in
a round, their fearsomeness and thrill, their reward and punishment.
They generally offer a fair test and a relatively safe way to play the
hole for most players, but they also arouse our imagination and tempt
the daring with more aggressive options. They are often the signature
holes on their courses, conveying the essence of the entire layout and
providing the most lasting memory of a round no matter how well one
plays this hole.

But more. *They get in our head.*

We know they are coming in our round. We may even get an
occasional glimpse of them from other locations on the course as our
round progresses. If they are late in a round, often deep in the back
nine where matches will be decided and a round either crowned or
ruined, the anticipation can be almost unbearable. Trouble lurks, and
it cannot be avoided. The "Road Hole" seventeenth at the Old Course
at St. Andrews, the eighteenth at Pebble Beach, the eighteenth at
Merion, the sixteenth at Cypress Point, the "Redan" fifteenth at North

Berwick, the seventeenth at Baltusrol's Lower Course, the seventeenth at Carnoustie—the list is long, impressive, and debatable.

Yet in a world of some thirty-three thousand courses and about a half a million holes, none may be more dramatic, more terrifying, and more recognizable than the par 3 seventeenth at the Tournament Players Club at Sawgrass in Ponte Vedra Beach, Florida. It is the signature hole on Pete Dye's spectator-oriented Stadium Course, home to the PGA's annual Tournament Players Championship. If, as Ben Crenshaw once said about the course, "It's *Star Wars* golf designed by Darth Vader," then the seventeenth is the "Death Star," a creation capable of annihilating planets, or at least foursomes.

First, it is an "island" hole, completely surrounded by a lake except for a narrow umbilical cord of a pathway at the back of the green, which is its only means of access for the players. It is not the first par 3 "island" green in the game and perhaps not even the hardest. A strong case for the latter can be made, for example, for the 193-yard "Moat Hole" at A.W. Tillinghast's 1917 design Galen Hall in Wernersville, Pennsylvania. Its tiny putting surface is surrounded by a 15-foot wide moat with 10-foot high banks and is accessed by a wooden foot bridge. Or perhaps the fourteenth at Coeur d'Alene in Idaho. This is a true island green of some 15,000 square feet. It is a man-made island and can play over 200 yards depending on the tees and where the "island" is anchored each day. It is only accessible by boat.

But there is no tee shot in golf more visually intimidating than what seventeen at Sawgrass offers. The ultimate stadium venue, it sits exactly in the middle between the sixteenth green and eighteenth tee with high grassy banks for spectator viewing overlooking it. It affords no bail-out option, no margin for error, no area for recovery. It is all or nothing.

Second, it is vulnerable to very high winds that can sweep across the course and the open lake. When the winds are up, as they were for the 1984 PGA Championship at Sawgrass, the stroke average for the hole was 3.79, the highest ever recorded for a par 3 at a PGA event. A total of 64 balls struck by the finest golfers in the world found the water from only 132 yards away. Those 64, though, are only a fraction of the 100,000-plus balls each year that are fished out of the lake.

And third, it is devilishly controversial. Has Pete Dye improved on nature or violated it? Is the hole a work of genius or a Frankensteinian horror? Is it a grotesque gimmick or a true test? How one fares on the hole may indeed influence how one answers such questions, but one thing is for sure—it is an unforgettable experience and worth a check on any golfer's bucket list.

32

Harmony

She graces them well,
seasons of balance and tone—
spring, fall, Merion.

WHEN LEE TREVINO won the U.S. Open at Merion in 1971, defeating Jack Nicklaus in an 1eighteen-hole playoff for the championship, he exuberantly declared, "I love Merion—and I don't even know her last name." Nicklaus has been no less effusive in his appreciation of the venerable course out on Philadelphia's Main Line. "Acre for acre," said Jack, "it may be the best test of golf in the world."

Consistently ranked in the top 10 among the world's greatest courses, Merion has charmed and challenged players of all stature and ability in the game for over a century ever since its East Course opened for play in 1912 amid reviews declaring it "the finest inland links in the country." Nineteen United States Golf Association championships, the most of any course in the nation, have been contested at Merion and underscore its enduring greatness.

Philadelphia's weather permits play on the course virtually year-round, and there is a hearty band of members who will play as long as the greens are not frozen and the grounds are not covered with snow. But the course is at its best in the spring and fall. For these are the seasons of grace, harmony, and transition, and they are perfect metaphors for a course that embodies these qualities so eloquently in its design and play.

As spring effects a shift from the harsh months of winter to the kinder seasons ahead and autumn provides both welcome relief from the notorious East Coast summer heat and humidity and a richly hued passage to the golfing off-season, the journey across Merion's 126 acres is replete with transitions and traditions, balance, and seamless harmony.

Leaving the tee and heading up the fairway of the long par 5 second hole, entirely bounded on the right by Ardmore Avenue, you can glance to your left and see across four holes. It is a grand view, reminiscent of true links land courses in Scotland, such as Muirfield or North Berwick, but it is an illusion of openness. For the narrow fairways are separated by thick bluegrass and fescue rough, a meandering creek affecting play on all four holes, and a few of Merion's famous 125 "white faces" bunkers with raised lips on the back side toward or next to the greens.

This scene is juxtaposed with the cloistered corners of the course at the greens on holes eleven and seventeen. The former is set in an amphitheater of trees on one side and a steep bank across Cobbs Creek on the other. The latter rests in a natural hollow surrounded by a rugged dunes scape of mounds, Scotch broom, and deep bunkers. These holes are as splendid in their isolation as they are reflective of the integrative design genius of the course and its timeless appeal.

Merion has often been described as three courses in one or, more precisely, a single play with three complementary storylines. An initial set of six holes dubbed "Drama" unfolds the character of the course, beginning with the first tee and its intimidating close proximity to the dining terrace and an immediate challenge to the golfer to choose a path to the green wisely. A middle stretch of seven holes averages less than 300 yards, earning the nickname "Comedy." It is anything but a joking matter. And then the final five with the crushing label "Tragedy." It requires forced carries toward an out-of-bounds roadway on two holes and negotiating an old rock quarry three times, including the par 3 seventeenth and par 4 eighteenth, which played 246 and 521 yards, respectively, in the third round of the 2013 U.S. Open.

What is perhaps Merion's ultimate statement about balance and harmony is that the course brilliantly reflects each of the three primary "schools" of golf architecture: strategic, heroic, and penal. And sometimes on a single hole. The transition from one to another is as subtle as the change of seasons, but it is distinct.

And therein is Merion's greatness. For a round here promises a journey through the varied landscapes and rich memory of golf. It connects players to the very origins of the game and its embrace of the natural elements that have shaped and affected it. This is an American beauty offering quiet, true affirmation every day to architect Pete Dye's judgment that "Merion is not great because history was made here. History was made here because Merion is great."

33

Children First

The game envisioned,
swiftly paced and quickly played—
heed the children's play

T HE COASTAL VILLAGE of North Berwick sits along the shore of East Lothian at the southern point of entry to the Firth of Forth off the North Sea. Like all of East Lothian, "officially the sunniest area of Scotland," as the visiteastlothian.org website proudly informs its readers, North Berwick is rich in history and the memory of its past. This included its place as a fashionable resort destination in the late nineteenth century with a reputation as the "Biarritz of the North."

Caravan parks and B&Bs have replaced the grand old hotels as the principal places of accommodation, and the indoor Leisure Pool at nearby Dunbar, with its flume and wave machine, has eclipsed the harbor pool at North Berwick as a recreational facility. But there is nothing shabby about the setting. Spectacular Bass Rock and three lesser crags form a stately gray line in the water offshore, the ruins of Tantallon Castle cast their own shadows into the sea, and Berwick Law, a 663-foot-high, cone-shaped volcanic hill, overlooks the entire scene.

There is nothing sorry about the golfing scene either. In fact, far from it. The scene includes four public putting greens and two eighteen-hole links courses, including the West Course of the North Berwick Golf Club. Currently ranked among the top fifty in the world by *Golf Digest*, the course has been steadily rising in the rankings, a highly deserved recognition for the quality and appeal of a course that is second only to the Old Course at St. Andrews for continuous play at one site.

Bordering the fifteenth and sixteenth holes of the West on the return to the clubhouse and protected from them with out-of-bounds stakes is one of the great surprises, among so many, at North Berwick. This is the "Children's Golf Course," and as its first rule clearly states, "Children have priority on the tee."

It is sheer delight to observe what goes on there. Carrying starter sets or just an assortment of pared-down clubs in their light bags, boys and girls ages six to twelve scamper across the few acres of the course and its nine holes ranging in length from 60 to 120 yards. Heeding a posted rule to "walk quickly between shots," they waste no time taking their swings or pursuing their consequences. No labored preshot routines, no agonizing debates over club selection, no tossing blades of grass into the air to gauge a breeze stiff enough to knock you over, no mummified poses plumbing putts. Yet in their nerveless haste, they never seem to fail to replace a divot, repair a pitch mark, or smooth a bunker.

Both the pace and practice of their play reflects the joy these children have discovered in this game and the factors that have made it possible. The Children's Course signals to the town's young people, as well as its adults and visitors, the importance of golf in this community. Like the public putting greens and the eighteen-hole courses, this facility is a matter of local pride and identity. It underscores the historical reputation of the game in North Berwick and its place in the region's economy. But more than these messages, the various golfing grounds here—none more so than the Children's Course—are an acknowledgment of the town's responsibility to foster the national culture.

A ten-year-old girl swinging her father's sawed-off, hand-me-down seven iron is hardly making a political statement in the way that her ancestors did when using golf as a symbol of irredentist patriotism after the union of England and Scotland in 1707. However unconsciously, though, she is engaged in a socializing exercise that is both cultural and developmental. The former affirms her heritage and the latter a set of values that are deemed important for the community and her own well-being. The Children's Course underscores her right of participation in a game that, through its nature and on these grounds, represents an historical treasure and encourages such virtues as responsibility, self-reliance, and rectitude. An "honesty box" on the first tee immediately communicates the importance of integrity to the game in collecting the two-pound greens fee when no attendant is present. The course also encourages a swift pace—and invites children to lead the way in showing how the game is meant to be played.

34

Primeval

What a charming scene,
golfers among the grazers—
the game primeval.

T HE COASTAL VILLAGE of Brora sits at the base of the Sutherland hills about fifteen miles north of Dornoch along the eastern edge of the Scottish Highlands. This is pasture land, where sheep and cattle so greatly outnumber their human neighbors that the constructed properties of the latter seem even more an invasion of the natural landscape than they normally would be.

The sheep, predominantly high woolen yield Scottish Blackface and Cheviot breeds, were not always as ascendant. They came with the Highland Clearances of the late eighteenth and early nineteenth centuries when the aristocratic, often-absentee landlords evicted their tenants and gave their estates over to sheep farming. The low stone walls along the A9 roadway from Inverness to Thorso and across the fields on either side are relics of a time when the land was divided into grazing parcels. Whatever ancient resentments may have existed between man and sheep, a harmony borne of interdependence and shared history now seems to prevail. And golf is one of its beneficiaries.

The common ground of this interaction includes the links of the Brora Golf Club. Originally a nine-hole layout dating to 1891, the course expanded to eighteen holes in 1923 upon the recommendations of James Braid, a five-time winner of the Open who had become one of the leading representatives of golf's Golden Age of course design after his playing years. He happily discovered that the course he was commissioned to improve was located on a broad stretch of gently rolling green fescue and straw-top bent grass above a dazzling white beach of the North Sea. It was ideal for two activities: grazing and golfing. As in Braid's day and earlier, these activities are carried out today simultaneously and contiguously, although it is clear that the sheep prefer one endeavor and humans the other.

It is also clear and particularly charming how the habits of the grazers have influenced the game of the golfers and effected a response that preserves their mutual claims on the land. Both users of this space have equal access to it. The sheep wander freely; the golfers only somewhat less randomly. The only restriction on the sheep is a two-foot-high fence strung with low-voltage electric wire that surrounds each of the tees and greens to keep the grazers from wandering upon them. The fence plays as an immovable obstruction and allows any shot striking it to be replayed without penalty.

Otherwise, the sheep are present either in small groups, which occasionally require negotiation, or in the evidence of their passage: well-trodden pathways throughout the course, closely cropped rough, naturally deposited loose impediments (treated in the same way as casual water), and a few primitive bunkers, which they have fashioned in the dunes to hunker down against the elements. Truly, the essential delight of Brora is as much Braid's pleasant design as it is the primeval golfing experience it provides.

That experience extends to a certain "back to the future" manifestation at some noteworthy new designs. These include, for example, Whistling Straits in Kohler, Wisconsin, three times since 2004 the site of the PGA Championship, and Machrihanish Dunes, which occupies the same dunes land on the Kintyre Peninsula of west Scotland as its famous neighbor, the Old Tom Morris–designed Machrihanish Golf Club. Both courses employ sheep not just as an ornamental feature, but as an integral part of their design, contributing to both their environmental and sporting success. Their sight is both a glimpse at the origins of the game and loving homage to the grazers and golfers of centuries' past who shared common ground.

35

Scottish Gothic

Fixed in time and place,
among the Danes and the dunes,
a count and a course

WHILE ON A walking tour along the northeastern coast of Scotland between Aberdeen and Peterhead in 1893, Bram Stoker happened upon the ancient fishing village of Cruden Bay. Stoker was on holiday, seeking quiet time and inspiration for a new novel he was considering. Cruden Bay provided both. Framed by the distant Braemar Mountains, its neat rows of cottages and red-tiled drying sheds tucked among the sandhills and meadows, the village seemed as isolated in time as it was in place. On these walks Stoker often carried a copy of *In a Glass Darkly*, a collection of short stories by the best-selling mystery writer, J. S. LeFanu. Stoker was particularly interested in a story entitled "Carmilla," a tale of vampirism.

Cruden Bay fascinated Stoker with both its rugged natural setting and history, especially its ties to the times of Malcolm and Macbeth. The meaning in its name—"blood of the Danes"—suggested part of this history. Perhaps the most chilling tie to its past was the ancient ruins of Slains Castle, sitting on the edge of the cliffs on a rocky point just southeast of the village center.

Slains was the ancestral home of the Errolls, one of Britain's oldest families. They established their claims to this land over a thousand years ago and then fought ceaseless battles to hold on to it. The invading Danes especially felt their wrath, falling before the swords of the Errolls and the army of Malcolm II, king of the Scots, in the Battle of Cruden in summer 1012. Centuries of struggles, political intrigue, terrible fights, early deaths, exiles, and beheadings followed. Exhaustion and attrition finally capped this bloody saga in the sixteenth century, and the Errolls abandoned Slains. What remains are the ghosts and the ruins—the stuff of imagination.

The gray walls and towers of Slains, overlooking the jagged coast, the tempestuous sea, the ancient battlefield, and a village decidedly more feudal than Victorian, completed the picturesque image that Stoker had been seeking for a key setting in his novel, namely, the home of its protagonist. For this was a place of gruesome memory and mystery. This was the castle of Count Dracula.

In the shadow of Slains is another expression of Scottish gothic imagination. Stretching southward beneath the castle promontory, across dunes land of rare splendor and macabre character, is the Cruden Bay Golf Course. Although golf was likely played across this landscape as early as the 1790s, it was not until 1926 that Tom Simpson accomplished the present design. He had been engaged to reimagine the original 1899 layout of Old Tom Morris and Archie Simpson, who had been commissioned by the Grand North of Scotland Railway to build a course as part of a holiday resort complex.

Against the backdrop of the slate gray waters of the North Sea, Simpson's links provide a majestic view. Huge sand dunes rise sixty feet and higher above the floor of the course. Thin ribbons of gorse-lined fairway cut through the steep, shaggy ridges. Some greens sit perched high upon the dunes, others hidden in their folds, hard by burns, and snug within dells. From an overlook that would eventually become the tee of the tenth hole, Stoker saw in the jagged reaches of the coastline the jaws of some fantastic monster, which lured ships to their destruction on the rocks below. It is not a comforting image.

But nothing about Cruden Bay is either passive or ordinary. It is unique and bizarre, the former characteristic reflecting the great variety among links land designs, the latter encouraging a cult following. Perhaps the most colorful and creative designer of his era, Simpson appreciated the rich fabric that this landscape provided to fashion his course.[26] Like a skilled cloth merchant, he unfolded it slowly, inviting buyers to feel the quality before revealing its pattern. At Cruden Bay, though, one is never quite sure that the next turn of the bolt will sustain the pattern that seems to be emerging. Like the brilliant slubs that enrich a tapestry and mark various transitions in its narrative, Cruden Bay shifts from dunes land classic to antiquarian quirky to post-modern shock.

Yet its eccentricity and mischievousness—its signal bells, directional posts, a bathtub-shaped green (complete with a "soap dish" bunker), mountainous sandhills, burial mounds of the vanquished Danes, and disconcerting hole names such as "Crochdane" ("Slaughter of the Danes"), "Bluidy Burn," and "Coffins"—underscore its charm just as its wild beauty defines its identity. There is a touch of madness here too, a reflection of Simpson's view that "it is only the mad masterpieces that remain in the memory." For golfers who seek the gothic or cutting edge or any expression in between, Cruden Bay is a place of fertile imagination, lasting memory, and true majesty.

36

Lahinch

Alert in its den,
the old fox hears the ball land—
and claims a new prize

ACCLAIMED BY HERBERT Warren Wind as "the St. Andrews of Ireland," the old town of Lahinch sits on the west coast of Ireland, about midway between Galway Bay and the River Shannon. Long a tourist mecca for those who came to see the Cliffs of Moher, walk the Burren, or find healing in the many holy water wells of the region, the town boosted its appeal with the addition of a golf course in 1892.

Members of the Black Watch Regiment stationed in nearby Limerick, had recognized the potential for establishing a wonderful links within the mountainous dune country lining the shore of Liscannor Bay. The man they asked to lay out the course, Old Tom Morris, agreed. For one pound and travel expenses, Old Tom completed the task quickly. For other than designating locations for tees and greens, he felt there was little else he needed to do. "I consider the links as fine a natural course as it has ever been my good fortune to play over," he proclaimed to the satisfaction of the local chamber of commerce.

The course added to its designer pedigree when it engaged Alister Mackenzie in 1927 to suggest some improvements to accommodate the greater distances achieved with the new rubber-core balls. Perhaps his greatest contribution was to place all eighteen holes within the dunes and to leave untouched two of Morris's most whimsical gifts to the golfing world, "Klondyke" the fourth and "Dell" the fifth. With their crossing fairways, blind shots, and straddling dunes, these holes provide a window on another era when such design features were in vogue.

The curiosities and charms of Lahinch also include its four-legged residents. The most famous are a small herd of devil-eyed Burren goats, which have been grazing on the course for over a hundred years. Like the sheep at Brora or Westward Ho! at North Devon in England, they have work to do. Yes, they crop the high grass, but the Lahinch goats also predict the weather. For attached to an old broken barometer on the clubhouse wall is a sign, "See goats." It directs golfers to check on the whereabouts of the goats in order to gauge the weather. If they are out roaming the dunes, the prospects for a clear weather day are strong. If they are huddled under the lee of the clubhouse near the first tee, not so promising. At least for goats.

The goats are not the only native fauna living among the dunes and providing entertainment at Lahinch. Often glimpsed upon the course are hedgehogs, hares, badgers, sloats, and fox. Most notably, a small red fox has inhabited a burrow dug into the steep sod wall of the right greenside bunker of the tenth hole. This is a stout par 4 of 441 yards to start the back nine. Requiring a solid tee shot to the right side of the fairway, it meanders left through a valley of dunes eventually reaching a well-protected, undulating, raised green. Two deep bunkers guard the narrow entrance to the green, the one on the right side located a few yards short of the putting surface at the bottom of a swale. It is in this bunker where the fox has set up home—and established claims on any ball hit there.

It is not uncommon for a player to arrive at this bunker to discover the fox sitting next to his ball. And not appearing too happy about the rude intrusion on his space. This situation begs a solution: either persuade the fox to move and relinquish the ball or invoking a hazardous condition clause in the rules, abandon the ball. More often than not, respect—or fear—of the fox prevails. The ball is lost, but a great story and memory gained.

Such are the many joys of Lahinch. "Savage as a tiger when the wind blows, mild and lovely on a sunny day," described John Burke about his home course where he won many of his Irish amateur championships in the 1930s and 1940s. The great champion may well have been describing Ireland herself. Indeed, an anonymous Irish cleric writing in the sixteenth century marveled how "the broom of Nature swept all the elements of heaven and earth so sweetly and intensely across the land." Nature's gifts at Lahinch include goats that foretell the weather and an ornery old fox that tests a player's patience and sense of humor. They are part of a scene where it seems every characteristic and creature of the course both underscore the harmony between history and nature there and contribute to an unsurpassed golfing landscape and an unforgettable playing experience.

37

Pilgrimage

*Stretched along the firth,
dunes splendid in golden bloom—
a pilgrim's reward*

UPON VISITING THE links of Royal Dornoch Golf Club for the first time, the American architect Pete Dye noted that "if an old Scot in a red jacket had popped out from behind a sand dune, beating a feather ball, I wouldn't have blinked an eye." For here, along the coastline of Embo Bay off the Dornoch Firth, is a course that sits in such wondrous isolation that it possesses, as Dye discovered, an aura of agelessness.

As far back as 1630, Sir Robert Gordon, the St. Andrew's educated tutor to the Highland's House of Sutherland, hailed the Dornoch links as "the fairest and largest of any part of Scotland." Its great rippling fairways, devilish bunkering, fierce trouble in the gorse-filled rough and whimsical mounding that guards the many naturally plateaued greens recalled the venerable links of the Old Course with which he was very familiar. Yet for most of its history, this extraordinary links, so far north that it sits on the same latitude as Juneau, Alaska, existed more as rumor than actual experience for the golfing world.

But there was strong evidence that something special resided on the eastern links land of the Central Highlands. In 1909, a small contingent of players from Dornoch so distinguished themselves at the British Amateur Championship at Muirfield that their performance was hailed as "the Dornoch Invasion." They inspired the first wave of pilgrims to visit the course where the Dornoch men had honed their games.

The word about Dornoch's qualities and appeal most fully spread through the work and influence of Donald Ross, a Dornoch native who had started his career in golf as a nineteen-year-old club maker at the town's course in 1891. John Sutherland, the club's longtime secretary and part of "the Dornoch Invasion," recognized Ross's talents and encouraged him to move to St. Andrews to apprentice with Old Tom Morris. Two years later, Ross returned to Dornoch as the club's greenskeeper and professional.

With such mentors as Sutherland and Morris, Ross learned a lot, but the strongest influence on his education was the links of Dornoch itself. His design career spanned five decades, but it started at Dornoch with modest improvements to the course mainly to accommodate the longer flying rubber-core ball. Whether his canvas was the sandy soils and piney woods of the Carolinas, the mountain slopes and valleys of Colorado, or the suburban parkland of southeastern Pennsylvania, Ross worked the native influences and strategic design philosophy of Dornoch into the approximately six hundred courses that he and his design empire developed. Not all his courses are equally great, to be sure, but they all reflect a continuity of purpose that both incorporates the natural landscape and resonates a touch of links land.

Ross was in the vanguard of the Golden Age of course design and influenced another wave of interest in Dornoch before the Great Depression and the Second World War. During the *fin de cycle* and early twentieth century decades, the golfing scene at Dornoch rivaled North Berwick in East Lothian as a holiday destination for the game's upper crust. The cataclysms of the 1930s and 1940s took their toll on the game everywhere. But once again, Dornoch found agents for its promotion that set the course on a pathway of greater renown and appreciation.

PAUL ZINGG

This time, Dornoch's champion was an American-born and Cambridge-educated writer for the *New Yorker*, Herbert Warren Wind, who first visited Dornoch in 1963 on a golfing holiday after covering the Walker Cup matches at Turnberry. Rare among Americans who have celebrated the virtues of seaside courses, Wind followed the advice of friends who insisted that these distant links, though far off the beaten track for most visitors to Scotland, were worth a visit. What he found and described in a memorable *New Yorker* article was "the most natural course in the world. No golfer has completed his education until he has played and studied Royal Dornoch."[27]

The majesty of the links and the splendor of its setting engage players from the very first tee—and never desert them. The outward holes make brilliant use of a border ridge that is absolutely spellbinding with the yellow gorse ablaze in bloom in the early summer. The course occupies three levels that sweep along the white sandy beach, occupy a raised plain above the beach holes but beneath the western ridge, and run along a narrow corridor at the top of the ridge. The eighth hole actually engages all three levels as the second shot on this 434-yard par 4 plunges across an old quarry and a moonscape of hummocks and bunkers to the green near Embo Point. It is a hole—like so many on this brilliant course—that rewarded Wind with "all that I hoped it would be—a thoroughly modern old links with that rare equipoise of charm and character that only great courses possess."

Although better bridges and roads make it somewhat easier now to get to Dornoch than Wind's time, the area lacks the transportation and accommodations infrastructure that severely restricts its likelihood of hosting an Open, but that does not prevent many of the Open participants from making the pilgrimage to Dornoch when they are in Scotland—or from considering what a wonderful Open it would be on these grounds. In that regard, this most northerly located course among the world's greatest is still a place for the imagination.[28]

38

Triumvirate, I

Trio of Britons,
fierce rivals and gentlemen,
scripting a new age

BETWEEN 1894 AND 1914, the Open Championship of Great Britain was conducted twenty-one times. Three men—Harry Vardon (6), John Henry Taylor (5), and James Braid (5)—combined to win the tournament on sixteen occasions. In each of the five tournaments over these years that neither of these men won the championship, one or more of them finished second. It was a record of dominance in one of golf's Majors unmatched before or since. The closest to their run was the performance of a more recent Big Three—Jack Nicklaus (5), Arnold Palmer (4), and Gary Player (3)—who won the Masters a combined twelve times in the twenty-one tournaments at Augusta National between 1958 and 1978.

Taylor was the first member of the Great Triumvirate to claim the Open championship, his initial triumph coming at Royal St. George's in 1894. His last occurred at Royal Liverpool in 1913, although he was a factor in the tournament until age fifty-five, when he tied for eleventh at Royal Lytham and St. Annes in 1926. He only competed in the U.S. Open once, finishing runner-up in 1900, but he won the French Open twice and the German once.

Braid won his five Open championships in one decade, 1901 to 1910, and was the last European player to win two successive titles in 1905 and 1906 before Padraig Harrington of Ireland successfully defended his 2007 title a year later. The Scotsman also won four British Match Play Championships between 1903 and 1911 and the French Open in 1910.

As distinguished the playing careers of Taylor and Braid, neither matched the record and reputation of Vardon. Admiringly called "The Stylist" or "Mr. Golf," and often introduced as "The Icon of Golfing," Vardon won another forty-two individual tournaments in addition to his six Open titles and one United States Open championship in 1900. He finished in the top 10 at the Open on eleven occasions and was runner-up at the U.S. Open by one stroke, each of the two other times he played in that event. One of those years was the watershed moment for American golf in 1913 at the Country Club when a twenty-year-old American amateur from Brookline, Massachusetts, Francis Ouimet, won the championship in a play-off with Vardon and Ted Ray, another Englishman. Vardon also won numerous team events representing Great Britain and England, including his countrymen's victory over a United States team in a 1921 match, which was a precursor to the Ryder Cup.

What these three champions of Great Britain achieved in and for the game, though, transcended what they accomplished as players. They not only accompanied the game into the twentieth century but effected so many key aspects of the culture and conduct of the modern game.

Taylor had already earned a high reputation as a clubmaker before he started his run of Open championships in the 1890s. As impressive his game and craftsmanship in the shop, it was Taylor's manner that underscored his greatest influence. He raised the image of the golf professional, turning, as Bernard Darwin wrote, "a feckless company into a self-respecting and respected body of men."

Braid too began his career in golf as a clubmaker but eventually found his stride as a player after he overcame years of frustration as a poor putter. His tournament playing career, though, was cut short by health issues and a decision to redirect his talents to course design. Among his more than two hundred designs or remodels are some of Great Britain's finest, including the king's and queen's courses at Gleneagles, Carnoustie, and Musselburgh. Like Taylor, he was also a founding member of the British Professional Golfers Association.

But again, it was Vardon who led the way in extending the sweep of the game from its clubbish nineteenth-century circles to an international stage. He did this primarily through his style of play. From perfecting a grip that allowed for more ball control and club speed to adopting a more upright stance and swing path that enabled him to hit the ball higher and land softer to his more patient and strategic approach to playing the game, Vardon demystified much about the game and made it more attractive for both current players and anyone just taking it up. Vardon's ball control was so remarkable that, as his nicknames suggest, it inspired a cult-like aura about him. Like Taylor and Braid, he was a remarkable gentleman who brought grace and respect to the game. Short of winning the United States Open in 1913, for example, nothing pleased him more than Ouimet's victory because he appreciated the humble American's grit as much as the boost to the game's popularity that his victory inspired.

Vardon, Taylor, and Braid—the Great Triumvirate. True superstars of their era, they not only ushered in the playing characteristics of the modern game but also its global reach. Appropriately so, they were all among the earliest members inducted into the World Golf Hall of Fame in the 1970s.

39

Triumvirate, II

The likes of greatness,
never seen before or since—
privileged their witness

OVER THE COURSE of eighteen professional golf seasons, 1958 to 1975, the trio of Arnold Palmer, Jack Nicklaus, and Gary Player won at least one of the game's Majors every year, but once. Nine times during this stretch, the players combined for two or more of the championships in a year. It was one of those multi-victory years, 1962, which set the stage for their emergence as the game's dominant threesome.

Palmer's victories in the Masters and the Open, combined with Nicklaus's first Major win at the U.S. Open and Player's triumph in the PGA championship, gave them a sweep of the four Majors that year. Their success rekindled the notion of a "grand slam," a term that journalist O.B. Keeler had summoned to describe the unique feat of Bobby Jones to win in a single year all four "major" events for which he was eligible to compete as an amateur, namely, the United States and British Open and Amateur championships in 1930. Ben Hogan came the closest after that in 1953 winning the year's first three professional Majors, but having to pass on the PGA because that event overlapped with the Open at Carnoustie.[29] But sharing the grand slam was enough for fans and the press to declare that in Palmer, Nicklaus, and Player, the era of the Big Three had begun.

And truly, there has never been—and may never be again—a contemporaneous threesome with such extraordinary achievements as players, sportsmen, and contributors to their game.

There were noteworthy "big threes," which preceded the king and his two fierce rivals and steadfast friends. The British trio of Harry Vardon, John Henry Taylor, and James Braid won seventeen Majors among them from 1894 to 1914, all Opens in Great Britain except Vardon's 1900 victory in the U.S. Open. Primarily in the 1920s, with the PGA Championship achieving status as a Major, Walter Hagen, Bobby Jones, and Gene Sarazen combined for twenty-five wins. And then, with the Masters added to the short list of Majors in the 1930s, Ben Hogan, Sam Snead, and Byron Nelson accumulated twenty-one Major titles from 1937 to 1954.[30]

But besides their greater number of titles, there was something special about how the Big Three of the '60s competed and how they endured. Nicklaus alone garnered eighteen Majors over a twenty-five-year span, 1962 to 1986. No one else comes close in terms of both titles and competitive longevity in these events. The average number of Majors and span of time between a first Major victory and last for the twelve other players with at least six Majors each are eight and thirteen, respectively.

Player, the "Black Knight" from Johannesburg, South Africa, accumulated 165 tournament victories over six continents in his World Golf Hall of Fame career. He is one of only five golfers—and the only non-American—to win all four Majors. Player's nine Major championships occurred over a twenty season span, 1959 (the Open, his first of three) to 1978 (the Masters, his third green jacket).

It was Palmer, though, who anchored the Big Three and was the catalyst of their rivalry and the interest it created. His seven Major championships came in a rush between 1958 and 1964, but no one brought more excitement to the game and more thoroughly captivated the golfing world's attention. Or earned the respect and fired the competitive juices of his rivals. Said Nicklaus: "My strongest motivation through all my best years wasn't the championships I won and the golfers I defeated, but those I lost and the players who beat me. If Arnold Palmer hadn't been there when I turned pro, I'm certain my record would have been a shadow of what I'm proud to have achieved." And Player: "The first time I saw Arnold Palmer I said 'There's a star.'"

Reflecting on the impact of the Big Three, two-time Masters champion Ben Crenshaw said simply, "They are our heroes. They truly represent what is best in our game, and what is best in us." Their scores of prestigious honors and distinctions over the decades—honorary university degrees, keys to cities, sportsman of the year selections, presidential commendations, lifetime achievement awards—echo Crenshaw's judgment. For these recognitions are as much about their success as players as they are their qualities as men of conscience and consequence, grace and class.

40

Glory

*A glorious light
flashes and fades with the flight
of the passing clouds*

WHEN BOBBY JONES won the U.S. Amateur at Merion in 1930, he completed what his biographer, O.B. Keeler, described as the "grand slam" of golf. This was a term that Keeler borrowed from bridge, and it signaled Jones's achievement of winning all four of golf's "major" tournaments in one year. In 1930, these were the U.S. Open and Amateur championships and the Open and Amateur titles in Great Britain. No one had ever done that before—and no one since.

The notion of a professional grand slam did not exist until the addition of the Masters tournament in 1934. It then joined the U.S. Open, the (American) Professional Golfers Association, and the (British) Open championships as the new, in Keeler's words, "impregnable quadrilateral." The modern grand slam had arrived. Beginning with Arnold Palmer's decision to compete in the Open in 1960 in order to add to the Masters and U.S. Open titles he had already won that year, the pursuit of the grand slam has been a gallant and captivating quest. Although five players—Jack Nicklaus, Tiger Woods, Ben Hogan, Gary Player, and Gene Sarazen—won all four Majors over the course of their careers, no one has won all four in a single year. Both Hogan (1953) and Woods (2000) came the closest with three in one year. Woods did hold all four titles at the same time, but over the course of two seasons, 2000 to 2001. His singular achievement has been dubbed the "Tiger Slam."

The mystique surrounding the grand slam events has ensured a place in the pantheon of golfing heroes for anyone who claims a victory in them. This is the case both for those 81 players who have won two or more Majors and for those 138 others who notched just one Major victory. For the former, more than one victory confirmed golfing greatness and, just as importantly, the legitimacy of the first title. For the latter, that single victory has often been both a blessing and a curse. When it came, it raised expectations of a golfing career ascendant with promise and glory. As the years went by without another grand slam triumph, many of the champions faced harsh judgment as suspect winners in a freakish event. Perhaps the cruelest cut in these cases was the view that a Major was not truly won by the champion but lost by the runners up.

There was nothing accidental, however, about the outcome of Jack Fleck's duel with Ben Hogan for the U.S. Open title in 1955 at the Olympic Club or Rich Beem's gritty performance in the 2002 PGA Championship at Hazeltine when he held off a fast-charging Tiger Woods. Hogan had all but been crowned with his fifth Open title with a final round 70 to take a two-shot lead over Fleck, who was still on the course. But three shots behind Hogan as the fourth round began, Fleck birdied two of his last four holes, including the eighteenth, to tie Hogan with a closing 67. He then outplayed him in the next day's playoff, 69 to 72. The Open was Fleck's first PGA tour win and his only Major.

Like Fleck, Beem battled the finest player of his era to a dramatic win. Playing in the group behind Woods in the fourth round, Beem watched Tiger birdie his final four holes to post a 9-under clubhouse lead. Yet just when all the world expected Beem to collapse under the pressure, he rolled in a thirty-foot birdie putt on the sixteenth hole and came home with a 68 to best Woods by a single stroke. Beem never won another tour event and made only nine cuts in his subsequent thirty-one Major tournaments.

For Fleck and Beem—and such other one-Major wonders as Todd Hamilton, Wayne Grady, Shaun Micheel, Orville Moody, Tommy Aaron, and Ben Curtis—glory rushed upon them. Yet there was little evidence in their careers up to the moment of their Major triumph that greatness awaited. And sadly, nothing extraordinary followed it.

Two others on this dubious list, David Duval and Ian Baker-Finch, especially struggled with the golfing world's expectations that they would be the game's next superstars. As their search for another win—any win—became more and more desperate, confusion and cluelessness about the state of their games effected a severe loss of confidence and put them in a free fall to become a mere footnote in the annals of the sport. The lowest moment for Baker-Finch probably came six years after his 1991 claret cup victory at Royal Birkdale, when, encouraged by many of his friends on the tour, he decided to play in the 1997 Open at Royal Troon. But this story did not have a fairy-tale ending. In the first round, he shot 92, twenty-one over par, the highest score in the field by five strokes. He subsequently withdrew from the championship and announced his retirement from tournament golf.

When he won the 1991 Open, Baker-Finch admitted that it had been difficult for so many years "visualizing winning, because I had lost so many times." Yet lately, he said after his win, he had been thinking "maybe I've finally paid all my dues." How cruel the years of missed cuts and futility that followed his brilliant closing rounds of 64–66, 10-under par, to claim the cup. How painful echoed the words of Bobby Jones: "No one will ever have golf under his thumb." Yet for one week, the debts were paid, and the clouds parted for the handsome Aussie with the can't miss game.

41

Old Head

O'er the raging deep,
a high and fearful vision
peers beyond the sea.

THERE ARE MANY approaches to Kinsale. Whether by land or sea, the routes to this port town overlooking the estuary of the River Bandon on Ireland's southern coast are among the most beautiful in the entire country. The coast road from County Kerry meanders southeast into County Cork past a succession of jagged peninsulas and rugged islands, large bays and deep inlets defining the untamed sea coast of Munster province. Ancient market towns sit on crossroads and at the heads of various waterways and reveal their once-strategic importance through the IRA memorials, castle ruins, and other archaeological sites that mark the landscape.

Out of Cork, the Irish Republic's second largest city, a shorter and more trafficked way to Kinsale heads southwest. It meanders through the valleys of the once-densely-wooded hills where druids performed their rites long before St. Finbar in the seventh century and the Vikings in the ninth settled upon the marshy island between two branches of the River Lee. Upon reaching Innishannon village, the Kinsale road turns due south and accompanies the River Bandon to the sea. Its many bends reveal one postcard view after another, each, it seems, complemented with its own weather and mood.

Yet there is unity within the transformation of atmosphere and scenery. Robert Lynd, writing a century ago, thought that the key element that provided a "personality" to Ireland and forged a connection among the vastly different Irish countrysides, was "the glory of light." Along the River Bandon road a multi-karat morning mist touches gently, brilliantly, equally on all it unfolds, especially the white-washed farmhouses and cottages of all shapes and sizes that dot the slopes and plains like so many yachts at anchor on a green sea.

Seven miles southwest of Kinsale harbor, where all manner of real sail and sporting boat come for the sun and blue shark, sits the Old Head promontory. It is a diamond-shaped tract of about Two hundred twenty acres connected to the rest of the peninsula and the mainland by a spectacular natural bridge. For eons, its rocky, exposed surface was a harsh landscape for various settlements. Until the brothers John and Patrick O'Connor, successful real estate developers and entrepreneurs with a sense that upscale golf and the Kinsale tourist business were made for each other, bought the land and covered it with thousands of tons of topsoil. What they imagined opened in 1997 as the Old Head Golf Links. There is nothing like it anywhere on the planet.

More cliff top in its character than either links style or headlands, the golfing grounds feature two-thousand-year-old castle ruins, standing stones, a mid-nineteenth-century lighthouse—the ruins of an earlier one from the seventeenth century—and a Frank Lloyd Wright-inspired clubhouse perfectly folded into a rocky slope at a high point on the course. They form a unique ensemble and glimpse into the peninsula's history, but they are just a side show for the main attraction, the course itself, and, more specifically, its nine holes that play completely along the edges of the cliffs three hundred feet above the pounding waves of the Celtic Sea.

It is nearly impossible to choose just one hole to exemplify what Old Head is all about. For truly just when you have played what seems to be the most spectacular golf hole in the world, you move on to another, but no hole better captures the Old Head experience than the par 5, 498-yard, dogleg left twelfth. Located on the more exposed western side of the peninsula, its tee sits on a sunken shelf carved into the cliff overlooking Ringagurteen Point. The northward drive to a narrow, semi-hidden fairway requires a thrilling transoceanic carry over the coves and caves of the sheer cliffs toward the distant towers of the castle ruins. It is a terrifying shot no matter how many times the hole has been played, and it captures everything the course offers—ancient ruins, vertiginous views, sweeping sea, cascading cliffs, and laugh-out-loud wonder.

As exciting and memorable an experience it is to play Old Head, the scene represents for many a troubling vision of the direction for golf in Ireland. Its three-hundred-euro greens fee for a weekend round, macadam cart paths and roaming bar carts, gated entrance, faux stone relics, year-in-advance reservation requirements, uniformed caddies, six tee boxes per hole, helicopter pad, and five-star restaurant with as many imported wines as native stouts and whiskeys suggest the tony dimensions of a new economy and value system. These attractions for the "discerning golfer," as the Old Head promotional materials unapologetically state, also question how far Ireland might roam from the more modest storylines of its national history and golfing culture. The answer will be in the lessons that others draw from Old Head and how the future of Irish golf bonds with its past. If past is prologue, it will be exciting to watch.

42

Greatness

Are cherry blossoms
more splendid than rose petals?
each in its own way

F OR OVER FIFTY years, golf magazines, writers, and commentators of the game in the United States, the United Kingdom, and elsewhere have provided ratings and rankings of golf courses. The best known of these are the biennial rankings produced by *Golf* and *Golf Digest* magazines. *Golf Digest* first published a list of "America's Toughest 200 Courses" in 1966, but by 1983 for *Golf* and 1985 for *Golf Digest*, the lists had emerged as "rankings." Subsequently, other guides in these matters have appeared, including *Golf Course Architecture* magazine and several European publications, including *Golf World*, *Golf Monthly*, and *Today's Golfer*.

A more esoteric source of this information and perhaps the most controversial and engaging is Tom Doak's *Confidential Guide to Golf Courses*. It achieved cultlike status as an underground publication in the 1980s before it made the mainstream with Sleeping Bear Press in 1996. It has since grown to a five-volume set covering more than 2,500 courses worldwide.

Although the leading rankings invite friendly debate among golfers and a fair amount of angst among clubs that have watched their rankings drop over the years, they follow a basic formula for determining notions of course greatness—as well as shaping a golfer's bucket list and fueling bragging rights. For the most part, this formula focuses on the *setting* and the *conditions* of play, and that begins with the design of the course and its success in holding the interest and challenging the abilities of those who play it.

As Doak explains and in the guidance that the editors of *Golf Digest* provide, the panelists who score the courses for their rankings, there is much agreement on the elements of course quality. To what extent do courses offer a variety of holes that balance risk and reward and test all aspects of a player's game? How clear is the evidence that a course is more than just a sequence of eighteen individual holes, that it is, in fact, a reflection of an integrated vision? How well does the routing and the scenic values of the course contribute to the enjoyment of the round and the memorability of the experience? How effectively does the course employ the natural contours of the land and engage the best features of the property on which it is built? Does play on such courses leave you with a sense of joy and satisfaction that comes with experiencing something truly special? How clearly can you recall the holes after a round? How eager are you to play the course again? Indeed, to what extent, says Doak about the few dozen courses on his list that earn a perfect 10, are these places that "stir our souls and will reward the visitor with something out of the ordinary."

Less easy to quantify but no less important to assessing quality is the ambience of a course. This criterion has more to deal with *feel* than physical evidence, but it clearly speaks to the *manner* of play that exists at courses and conveys much about both the state and nature of the game there. Is the game swiftly pursued, respectfully engaged, and delightfully shared? Is the *spirit* of the game and its traditional values evident in the history and appearance of the club through sportsmanship and care for the conditions of the course? Is the membership mindful of its responsibilities to ensure the quality of the course and the experience of the club for visitors?

Undoubtedly, there are clear and compelling reasons why, year after year, places such as Pine Valley, Augusta National, Cypress Point, Shinnecock, the Old Course at St. Andrews, and Royal County Down are consistently ranked at the top of the world's greatest courses. Anyone who has played these courses *feels* their greatness and enjoys a sense of privilege in being on their grounds.

Yes, *greatness* can be defined and witnessed, but it is also very personal, very much in the eye of the beholder. And that may have as much to do with the experience of the course as the memory of the occasion that initially brought a player to it. It also embraces the factors of long-term attachment to a particular place. This perspective invites different notions of greatness than those within the "official" guides and rankings, for it adds another layer to an endless debate, reveals that a great *course* and a great *experience* are not necessarily the same thing, and underscores how this game is such an intense personal experience as well as a shared one.

43

Old Tom

Here, there, tees and greens,
thirty-six stakes in the ground—
Old Tom finds a course.

H ORACE HUTCHINSON, AN accomplished English amateur golf champion of the late-nineteenth century who later turned to teaching and writing about the game, may have best captured the essence of Old Tom Morris when he praised him as "the common golfing ancestor" of the architects who flourished in the Golden Age of course design in the early twentieth century. After fourteen years as Keeper of the Green at Prestwick, Old Tom returned to the town of his birth, St. Andrews, in 1865 for the princely sum of fifty pounds a year and the title custodian of the links. For the next thirty-nine years, Old Tom took on the responsibilities of greens keeper, playing professional, club and ball maker, golf teacher, and course designer.

He achieved great success in all these roles, winning, for example, the Open Championship four times. The last of those victories occurred in 1867, when, at age forty-six, he became the oldest player to etch his name on the Claret Cup, but he undertook no endeavor more brilliantly or influentially than as a course designer. Ironically, it was an activity that he largely regarded as a hobby and for which he was often paid the grand sum of one pound a day to lay out a course.

Yet the allure of the Old Course and admiration for Old Tom directly influenced a particular style among the greatest designers in the history of the game who flocked like pilgrims to the old gray town in the Kingdom of Fife to spend some time with the grand old man. His visitors included Alister Mackenzie, Harry S. Colt, Charles Blair Macdonald, Donald Ross, Hugh Wilson, and Albert W. Tillinghast; and they in turn passed on what they had learned to their students: Bobby Jones, Seth Raynor, William Flynn, George C. Thomas, Chandler Egan, and Max Behr among many others. The family tree of golf design in the Golden Age spread its branches widely, but the ground in which it was planted was the Old Course, and its trunk was Old Tom Morris.

Old Tom's approach to laying out a new course basically reflected the standard practices of his era. Armed with thirty-six wooden stakes, he roamed the landscape planting them where he felt eighteen tees and greens should be located. For thanks to Tom and the Old Course, eighteen holes had become the rule for a full course by the late-nineteenth century; and like other course designers, he left the work of connecting the dots of the course he "found" to the club or town that engaged his services.

The keys to the lasting quality and example of his work were recognizing the potential of very different landscapes to yield space for the game and then, of course, deciding where to plant those stakes. Respect for the natural contours and features of the land, vision for its conversion to a golfing venue, and, most importantly, imagination guided his routing plans that were often bold departures from the traditional "loop" configuration of nine holes out and nine back along the same pathway. But more. Old Tom pioneered the basic principles of strategic course design and anticipated the effects that changes in club design and ball composition would have on the length of courses.

The evolution of the ball from featherie to gutta-percha to the rubber-core Haskell eventually made many of the courses he either designed or remodeled look and play very differently from his original layouts, but his touch is still there to be witnessed and appreciated at such places as Westward Ho!, Dornoch, Carnoustie, Prestwick, Muirfield, Machrihanish, Crail, Lahinch, Portrush, Rosapenna, Nairn, Cruden Bay, Royal County Down, and the Old, New, and Jubilee courses at St. Andrews. Just as surely, such individual holes as "Battery" the first at Machrihanish, "Dell" the sixth at Lahinch, "Foxy" the fourteenth at Dornoch, "Bluidy Burn" the sixth at Cruden Bay, "Burn" the first at the Old Course, and "Alps" the seventeenth at Prestwick reveal not only the brilliance of his vision but also the twinkle of delight and mischief in his eyes for what he fashioned.

Not surprisingly, Old Tom also contributed significantly to two complementary aspects of design—greens keeping and agronomics. As with his design work and with not much else than "a wheelbarrow, spade and shovel," as he famously told the story, Old Tom brought the world of golf into the modern age through such techniques as top-dressing greens, cutting and smoothing putting surfaces with push mowers and rollers, establishing separate teeing areas for each hole, locating yardage markers on holes, and managing the placement and condition of hazard areas. Each move was an innovation—and each lasted. Each underscored the legacy of the beloved gentleman who transformed the game and won the hearts of countless admirers.

44

Design

The art of design,
joining the game to the land—
Mackenzie at work.

HIS WORK SPANNING four decades, four continents, and nearly four hundred courses, including three consistently ranked among the world's top 10 (Augusta National, Cypress Point, and Royal Melbourne), Alister Mackenzie ushered in the Golden Age of golf course design in the early twentieth century. Although other important designers had preceded him, most notably Old Tom Morris, James Braid, and Harry S. Colt—the latter who was the first landscape architect to devote his career entirely to designing golf courses—none eclipsed Mackenzie for the quality of his work and his influence on the shape and spirit of the game's playing grounds.

Born in Yorkshire, England, in 1870, Mackenzie brought a simple formula to his work that he executed faithfully and brilliantly. It rested on two key principles. First, he respected what nature provided as the foundation for his courses. As he wrote in his influential 1920 treatise, *Golf Architecture: Economy in Course Construction and Green-Keeping,* "the chief object of every golf course architect worth his salt is to imitate the beauties of nature so closely as to make his work indistinguishable from nature itself." Second, Mackenzie championed the "strategic" school of course design that aimed to achieve interest, variety, challenge, and fairness for players of all abilities on his courses. Moreover, through routing and the balance among holes of varying lengths and character, he built courses designed to make use of every club in a player's bag.

Mackenzie's approach to course design was shaped by his keen ability to learn from what he observed. As a civilian doctor serving with the British army during the Boer War in South Africa, he was impressed with the camouflage techniques employed by the Boers to make the best use of natural cover to mask their movements and deployments. Similarly, as he said about the Old Course at St. Andrews, "the real reason [it] is infinitely superior to anything else is owing to the fact that it was constructed when no one knew anything about the subject at all, and since then it has been considered too sacred to be touched."

Mackenzie and the other great designers of his era also accomplished their work without the assistance of massive, mechanical earth-moving equipment. This is particularly evident in his design of greens and placement of bunkers. For the most part, he kept the natural undulations in the putting surfaces of his courses or manipulated them in subtle ways in order to emphasize their slopes and hollows and establish multiple locations for hole placements. Similarly, with bunkers and other hazards, he rejected the notion that they were there to "punish" poor shots. Their real object, Mackenzie explained, "is to make the game interesting." They should be placed with that purpose in mind in order to influence how the hole could be played.

What is truly remarkable about Mackenzie's courses—whether links land or park land, densely wooded valleys, rolling hill country, or open flat land—is the consistency and integrity of his design principles. Consider the stellar quality and great variety of these courses: the Old Course at Lahinch and Cork Golf Club (Ireland); the Portland Course at Royal Troon and the Rosemount Course at Blairgowie (Scotland); Crystal Downs (Michigan); Pasatiempo, the Meadow Club, the Valley Club, Fort Washington, and Haggin Oaks

(California); Royal Adelaide (Australia); Jockey Club (Argentina). It is an enduring legacy. The product, as Herbert Warren Wind described, of a man with "the soul of an artist, the brain of an engineer, and the heart of a golfer."[31]

45

Gorufu

Even in Tokyo
blossoms do not always grace
the golfing landscape

I N THE LAND of the original *haiku* poets, the quest "to be the ball" is struggling. On the surface, Japan has much to suggest a thriving golfing culture. Over six million Japanese (about 5 percent of the nation's population) pursue the game in a country that has about two thousand courses to play. Among all the world's countries, only the United States, with a population nearly threefold greater than Japan and six times the number of courses, has more players and courses.

The private golf club scene throughout the country is among the most expensive, competitive, and extravagant in the world. The exclusive Koganei Golf Club within Tokyo prefecture, for example, offers memberships for sixty-five million yen ($600,000), while others in the Tokyo area such as Yomiuri, Hachioji, Ome, and Tama are priced between twenty-five to forty-five million yen ($230,000 to 400,000). The great majority of Japanese golfers, though, find alternative venues to pursue their games; yet with only about a third of Japan's courses providing public access, many resort to driving ranges and indoor video simulators. The driving ranges, in particular, are legendary. In the country's major cities, the wait for a stall at a typical triple-decked facility can be an hour or more. At these facilities and elsewhere, Japanese golfers spend around $3 billion a year for equipment, and much of this is on products from such homegrown industry leaders in technology and global sales as Mizuno, Miura, Honma, XXIO, Fujikura, and Diamana.

The success of such male and female Japanese players on the world professional tours as Hideki Matsuyama, Hideto Tanihara, Yuta Ikeda, Naru Nomura, and Ai Miyazato further underscores the interest in golf in the country, although they are often regarded more as entertainers than professional athletes by the media. Still, the game will likely enjoy a boost with the 2020 Tokyo Summer Olympics and the gold medal competition at the East Course of the Kasumigaseki Country Club. Located about fifteen miles northeast of Tokyo, the course is one of Charles Alison's finest and has achieved something of a cult status for its cavernous bunkers and designer pedigree. For Alison was also the designer of three other Japanese courses—Hirono, Kawana (Fuji), and Naruo—which consistently earn spots on the world's top 100 lists.

As encouraging as these numbers and developments suggest for the game in Japan, there is a larger context that provides a more troubling picture. The number of players pursuing the game is now about half of what it was in the boom years from the late 1980s to early 1990s. During those years of extraordinary economic growth and investment speculation, the game attracted nearly a million new golfers a year, many of them caught up in the "company golf" craze that linked golf to both individual and corporate status and success. To accommodate these players, the number of courses in Japan increased by almost a thousand in the decade after 1983, peaking at 2,458 in 2003. Since 2005, however, Japan has seen an average of 50 courses a year close.

What accounts for these trends is a familiar story. Japan's baby boomers have moved away from a game that they view as too expensive and too time-consuming. Golf club memberships, which used to keep hundreds of brokers in Tokyo busy buying and selling them like stocks are available for a fraction of the prices they commanded during the boom years. At the prestigious Hourin Country Club, for example, memberships that went for $700,000 plummeted to $35,000. Golf course investors have found new buyers for their valuable lands, especially through conversion to solar farms. They have also discovered the tax benefits in such decisions because solar is not regarded as a "luxury" item as golf courses are.

How Japan finds a path forward for a game that has deep history and important socioeconomic meaning and consequence will be closely watched by countries and communities facing similar challenges. Already there is an emphasis on the "democratization" of the sport through lower greens fees and membership costs, campaigns to attract women and youth to the game, and other efforts to rid its elitist reputation and corporate culture vestiges. It is noteworthy that televised broadcasts of women's tournaments frequently attract greater viewership than those of the men. Whether this reflects a genuine appreciation for the quality of the ladies' play or merely affords a titillating experience for some of the male audience is a debatable matter, but it is evidence of a sport very much in flux.

A unique strategy in Japan to restore the game's standing might be an appeal to the gods, and there is a promising center for this effort at the Zenshoji temple located in Annaka-shi northeast of Tokyo. For here an enterprising temple priest has erected a six-foot-tall version of the Goddess of Mercy, who, with a putter in one hand and thirteen other golf clubs emanating from her head, greets golfers on the journey to more fairways and greens. As deities go, there is probably none more sympathetic to the plight of golfers. For this goddess, popularly known in Japan as *Kannon-san*, willingly chose to delay achieving Nirvana because she had so much compassion for the suffering of her supplicants.

So yes, there are golf gods, and there are the realities of shifting market forces and changing social habits—and golfers in desperate need of help for their game—and who is to say that *Gorufu Kannon-san* is not without some influence in these matters?

46

Game Changer

The outsider's child
chooses the path of daring
that comes from within.

A T A TIME when the highest levels of competitive golf were dominated by such great British champions as Harry Vardon, James Braid, John Taylor, and Ted Ray, when golf seemed an activity only for the affluent who pursued their games on elite private courses, a twenty-year-old son of a poor French-Canadian immigrant entered his first U.S. Open in 1913. Francis Ouimet was the last player admitted to the field at the Country Club in Brookline, Massachusetts, but it was a course that he knew well. For the humble frame house in which he lived with his parents and three siblings sat directly across the street from the club's seventeenth hole. From that vantage point, young Francis had closely observed the play of the club's better players and occasionally snuck on the course to try a few shots of his own.

His first shot of the tournament was a snap hook, which barely traveled forty yards. It led to a double bogey. It was followed by another double on the second hole. Four over par and six shots behind the opening round leader after only two holes, yet three days later, culminating in a decisive playoff victory over Vardon and Ray, Ouimet had accomplished "the most momentous win in all golfing history," according to one of its witnesses, Bernard Darwin, the renowned British golf writer.

No one had given this young amateur, whose only noteworthy win to date had been the Massachusetts State Amateur earlier that year, a chance. And for good reason. An amateur had never won the U.S. Open and only one American, John McDermott, had previously broken the stranglehold that the Brits held on the event since its inauguration in 1895. Yet both sides of the Atlantic hailed his triumph, for it was not just the courage of his game but the appeal of his manner that won the hearts and admiration of those who cheered his play and recognized what he had accomplished. In those few days, Ouimet turned the world of golf upside down.

Ouimet's victory was no less than a triumph for the masses. It liberated the American golfing scene from the notion that the game was "an amusement for the well-to-do classes alone . . . [in which] the poor man has no place," and it inspired countless aspiring golfers to imagine room in the game for themselves.[32] If a former caddie who carried the bags of the rich in order to help support his family, who rebelled against his father's wishes to drop out of high school and do "something useful" in his life, could reach the pinnacle of the sport in America, how could this game be denied to anyone? Within a decade of Ouimet's championship, the estimated number of golfers in the United States had increased sevenfold from around three hundred thousand to over two million. One of them was eleven-year-old Bobby Jones, who awaited in Atlanta, Georgia, that September day for word of Ouimet's fate in the playoff.

As much as the magnitude of his victory, what defined Ouimet's entire life after that was the magnanimity of his character. The grace and dignity with which he conducted himself throughout the tournament won lifelong admirers. One of them was Eddie Lowery, the ten-year-old caddie who was assigned to Ouimet because no other caddie was available. As Ouimet prepared for the playoff, a club member approached him and suggested that he should have a "real" caddie for the round. Ouimet politely declined, saying simply, "No, thank you. I'll stick with Eddie." He and Lowery remained friends the rest of their lives, much of it spent promoting American golf, especially the amateur game.

Ouimet followed his Open victory with two U.S. Amateur championships in 1914 and 1931, the French Amateur title in 1914, and eight consecutive appearances on the American Walker Cup teams from 1922 to 1934, all of which were won by the United States. He also captained four other American teams to victory, but pursuing a middle-class career as a banker, stock broker, and financial adviser, he never lived off his celebrity status and never considered becoming a golf professional. Instead, he allowed others to honor him for the good of the game. Most notably in this regard was the creation of the Francis Ouimet Scholarship Fund, a need-based college scholarship program for young people who had worked as caddies in Massachusetts.

Still, the honors came. In 1951, Ouimet was named the first non-British captain of the Royal and Ancient Golf Club of St. Andrews. He was an original inductee into both the PGA Hall of Fame in 1940 and, along with Bobby Jones, Gene Sarazen, and Walter Hagen, the World Golf Hall of Fame in 1974. In 1955, he was the first recipient of the Bob Jones Award, the highest honor bestowed by the United States Golf Association in recognition of distinguished service and sportsmanship in golf.

The recipient of so much credit and the inspiration for so many who challenged the game's exclusive culture, Ouimet most likely would have been content with Herbert Warren Wind's simple assessment of his life: "He was a great boy who became a great man." But in the closing words of his definitive history of the 1913 Brookline Open, Mark Frost tells us why:

> Everyone of us who casually or passionately plays
> the game for fun, companionship, competition or
> recreation should be forever grateful that Francis
> Ouimet looked out at that private, privileged world
> across the street from the house where he grew up,
> and found somewhere within himself the courage to
> cross the street.[33]

47

Seve

*The Euros rise to
the splendid light of genius—
Seve ascendant*

IN THE QUARTER century from Ben Hogan's triumph at Carnoustie in 1953 to Jack Nicklaus' second claret cup in 1978 at St. Andrews, only one European had won the Open Championship. This was Englishman Tony Jacklin at Royal Lytham & St. Annes in 1969. Several non-Europeans had claimed the title Golfer of the Year over this period, most notably Peter Thompson of Australia and both Bobby Locke and Gary Player of South Africa, but no one from either the United Kingdom or the continent. Similarly, there had been only one European winner of the U.S. Open during this stretch (Jacklin again in 1970) and never a European winner of either the Masters or the PGA Championship. The Euros fared just as poorly in the Ryder Cup, winning only one match in 1957.

And then a bolt of pure genius changed the scene and the odds.

Seve Ballesteros burst on the world golfing stage at the 1976 Open Championship at Royal Birkdale. The son of a Pedrena farmer from the north coast of Spain, Seve lived with his parents and three older brothers in a one-story house above the ground floor where they kept their cows, but he was raised on golf. His three brothers all became golfing professionals, albeit without much success as tournament players, yet they all recognized Seve's undeniable zest for the game and encouraged the development of his skills. He turned pro at age seventeen in 1974, although he was hardly known beyond the small world of Santander Bay.

The 1976 Open changed all that. Leading by two strokes over Johnny Miller after three rounds, Seve faded in the fourth with an errant driving round yet still finished second to Miller, tied with Jack Nicklaus six shots back. Miller's closing 66 was brilliant, and the cup was his, but the talk of the tournament was Seve. In many respects, this was his coming-out party. His audacious play from tee to green, seeming disregard for the potential disaster awaiting on some shots, and exquisite touch around the greens thrilled those who saw him play that day and fueled a sense that here was someone special.

For the next twenty years, Seve proved just how much so. Not only did he win tournaments—fifty European tour titles and eighty-seven victories worldwide, including five Majors (three Opens and two Masters)—but he did so with flair, joy, and a competitive intensity that willed his own success and revitalized the European Tour. He pulled his fellow European players upward with him, shattering so many glass ceilings along the way. Most notably, these included becoming the first European ever to win at Augusta in 1980 and turning the tide of European fortunes in the Ryder Cup.

The latter was built on a commitment to the event as a player, captain, and catalyst for the European resurgence in the event. He played on five winning Ryder Cup teams, including as non-playing captain in an emotional one-point victory in 1997 at the Valderamma Golf Club in Andalusia, Spain. Throughout his Ryder Cup career, he played with his fellow Spaniard and protégé Jose Maria Olazabel in fifteen matches, winning eleven of them, halving two, and losing only two at this pinnacle of international golfing competition. Overall, he tallied 22.5 Ryder Cup points in eight contests, ranking him fourth among all European players.

Back problems forced Seve to retire from the game in 2007, and a four-year bout with brain cancer eventually took his life in 2011. He brought to this final struggle the same kind of determination and courage that characterized his play.

In many respects, Seve was linked to another golfer whose legacy is so great that he is affectionately known by only his given name—Arnie. Like Arnold Palmer, Seve had his great contemporary rivals, including Nick Faldo and Tom Watson, who both won more Majors than he did. In Arnie's case, this was Jack Nicklaus whose eighteen Majors outshone Arnie's seven, but no one was more significant in American golf than Palmer. The same can be said about Seve for Europe. Said Bernard Gallagher, who captained Ballesteros in three Ryder Cups between 1991 and 1995: "America had Jack Nicklaus and Arnold Palmer—Seve was our Arnold Palmer and Jack Nicklaus rolled into one." Though hardly a saint with a volatile temper and shocking fallibility on occasion, no European player was more loved and revered.

48

Sense of Place

*Noon on the fence rail
the sparrows gather and spy
for the day's pickings*

T HE INTERSECTION OF Golf Place and the Links roads in St.
Andrews is one of the most iconic settings in the world of golf.
From this corner, approached from North Street through a narrow
corridor of shops and pubs, the great lawn of the adjoining first and
eighteenth fairways suddenly appears. The impact is startling. It is not
unlike the exhilaration felt by the spectators at an old inner city ballpark
when they emerge from the damp shadows of the entrance tunnels into
the dazzling sunlight to behold the perfect emerald playing grounds
before them.

For frequent visitors, this scene is firmly etched in their minds like so
many station stops along a familiar route. Turn left at the corner and
slip past the Old Course and Tom Morris shops and follow the row
of weathered stone buildings housing several of the town's many golf
clubs. The last in this line is the New Golf Club, and it sits almost at
the juncture of the Links and Old Station Road, directly across from the
Swilken Bridge. Go forward past the eighteenth green and toward the
first tee where the grand gray clubhouse of the Royal and Ancient Golf
Club looms over the scene. Behind the clubhouse stands the Martyrs
Monument, a ten-meter-tall sandstone obelisk commemorating four

Protestant reformers who were executed for their faith in the mid-sixteenth century. It sits on a high point of the Scores along with a stately line of homes, pubs, and B&Bs. They overlook the West Sands, celebrated in the opening sequence of the Academy Award-winning film *Chariots of Fire*, and beyond, the waters of St. Andrews Bay.

Yet those familiar with this scene need to resist the urge to point out everything to first-time visitors because so much of this place is personal, and it deserves an unfiltered introduction. Still, there are "secrets" to share and the satisfaction to have in providing some insider information to a friend. Just such a revelation is the low white fence that forms the out-of-bounds border along the right side of the eighteenth hole and extends around the green.

From late morning to dusk, the fence attracts spectators who lean and sit upon it as they watch the golfers finish their rounds. Many camp out there for lunch—and the entertainment. For this too is a sporting place—and the game is betting. The object of interest is the play of the golfers before them. Coins and pounds exchange hands on the outcome of a pitch, the prospects of an up-and-down from the Valley of Sin, the results of a six-foot putt. Quiet eruptions or groans signal the consequences of these moments. It is all great fun, if just a bit confounding to an unknowing player who may find herself being congratulated by a total stranger for a well-holed putt on the eighteenth green.

The fence is just another element of the Old Course scene that underscores its distinctiveness and memorability—its unique sense of place. These elements warrant discovery wherever they may be. The goats at Lahinch and the sheep at Brora. The lighthouse at Turnberry and the twelfth century watchtower at Tralee. The burger dog at the Olympic Club's halfway house and an "Arnold Palmer" at Arnie's own Bay Hill. The color-coordinated floral displays at Killarney and the broom ablaze in bloom at Dornoch. The view backward from the seventh tee at Gullen No. 1 to the nearby grounds of Muirfield and the glimpse of a Druid altar high in the woods to the right of the twelfth green at Druids Glen.

None of these features directly affect play on their courses, but all of them contribute to the memorability of rounds there. For as Yogi Berra, the Hall of Fame catcher for the New York Yankees, once said about baseball, "You can observe a lot just by watching."

This is every bit the case with golf. Location, setting, history, tradition, culture, folklore, legend—all those elements that *surround* the fields of play—deepen both the appeal and the mystery of the game. Yes, it bears watching—and seeing beyond the strokes, the grounds, and the moments.

DISCOVERY AND MEANING

49

Discovery

Look beyond the score,
renascence and reverie—
embrace the journey.

THERE MAY BE no more important goal in the pursuit of learning than self-discovery. Finding out about ourselves is a process that has as much to do with demonstrating one's will as it does taking a specific action. Reading, thinking, making friends, meditating, exploring foreign cultures, and chancing unfamiliar experiences are among the myriad of activities that cause us to look at ourselves in new and different ways. No less so, how we do in moments of stress when we have been pushed to our mental or physical limits reveals much about who we are.

Sport provides an infinite variety of these moments. They can be both grand and subtle depending upon the stage and the occasion. These moments abound in golf and underscore its appeal.

Standing for the first time on the first tee at the Old Course of St. Andrews, a lifelong dream come true, you yearn for a successful start to the round. Members of an ever-moving crowd of spectators just behind the tee have paused to watch (and judge) your swing. You imagine the faces of the membership of the Royal and Ancient Golf Club, past and present like Dickens's Christmas ghosts, peering through the high, dark windows of their clubhouse. They are not smiling. A few hours later, you arrive at the eighteenth green only a few yards away from where you started. The crowds and the ghosts are still there. Your match is all square, and you face a slippery, downhill five-foot putt to halve.

Can you keep your wits about you in such moments? Can you summon the knowledge of your skills and the recollection of times when you did so to play well in challenging circumstances? For this is a real learning experience, a lesson in self-discovery and self-mastery. Indeed, every such moment is as much about oneself as an opponent. The ultimate adversary is within.

If one of the reasons we play golf and other sports is to help us find out what kind of person we are, another is to help us become the kind of person we aim to be. In this regard, sports participation is both revelation and rehearsal.

Yet this is not a passive indulgence. It requires a commitment. It requires, in fact, a willingness to risk the outcome, to face activities and situations that are uncertain and unpredictable in what they will yield. It requires daring, something about which the American writer Eudora Welty reminded us we are all capable—because "serious daring comes from within."

To bring daring to this game—a demanding course ventured, a difficult shot attempted, a blustery day engaged, a tough match welcomed— acknowledges its nature and invites surprise. Wonder accompanies a game that not only reveals so much about those who play it but also offers so many marvelous possibilities in the consequences of its pursuit.

PAUL ZINGG

50

Seeing

What fills the spaces
between the targets and shots—
nothing, everything

Can you see the brook that golfers fear, and not fearing, but feeling, can you
put that flowing into your swing? The green grass restful to body, soothing
to soul. Is it so many paces that you put on it, or is it a period of rest and
calmness between you and the lie of the ball? Be the tree rooted, be the brook
flowing, be the calmness of the green.

—From the notebooks of Shivas Irons in *Golf in the Kingdom*

WHAT'S IN A golfer's mind when preparing to hit a shot? Dread, doubt, fear—or confidence, optimism, joy? The most recent tip seen on the Golf Channel or read in a golf magazine—or the jumble of countless clues to a better game accumulated over an entire golfing life? The technical precision and athleticism of a twenty-something tour pro—or the awkward pass at the ball by a thirty-plus handicap playing partner? Relishing the challenge of the shot at hand—or wishing the day's ordeal would just end? Or perhaps nothing to do with golf at all, just a mind wandering to the office or the daily news or the unpaid bills.

The *inner game* of golf, as is the case for all sports, focuses as much on the attitude that a player brings to the endeavor as its physical requirements. This focus is largely a reminder that mind and body are one and that they effect both proficiency in the game and the enjoyment of its pursuit. The kind of perspective that Shivas Irons taught, however, does not promise the immediate transformation of a poor game to strokes of genius; but it does underscore that a healthy mind-set guides the body, much more so than the reverse, and that a head filled with bad images will in all likelihood yield a scorecard filled with bad numbers.

What constitutes a healthy mind-set are a number of elements straight out of Norman Vincent Peale's playbook for "positive thinking": always aim to play your best, embrace the challenge, trust your abilities, focus on what is possible, raise your expectations, commit to an orientation on process rather than results, resolve to change your world through changing your thoughts, and recognize that "what the mind can conceive and believe, and the heart desire, you can achieve."[34]

This is a prescription for building confidence *and* competence with so much of it hinging on and connecting to the ability to focus on a target and visualize its attainment. This is what visualization in golf is all about, and it may be, as Nick Faldo has said, "the most powerful tool" that a golfer has.

Among the many reasons why golf is a hard game is the fact that a player is not actually looking at the target when a ball is struck. As the swing begins and as it progresses through and beyond the immediate moment of impact, the target is actually in the mind's eye; and in the simplest argument for developing the skills and discipline of visualization, unless the mind has a clear idea of the target and the pathway to it, the brain's communication with the body's muscles to pull off the shot will not be sure. Lacking preparation for the shot and clarity for its requirements, it is not surprising that a swing will fail to accomplish its goals. For if a golfer's mind is consumed with a checklist of mechanistic "swing thoughts" and other distractions, the brain will be preoccupied with other matters besides what is most crucial, that is, alerting and activating the precise muscles necessary to execute the shot.

Visualization is also a pathway to creativity. For it invites the mind to *create* pathways to the targets throughout a round. It adds another tool to a golfer's game—imagination.

Like any other aspect of a player's game, developing visualization skills requires practice and repetition. They are honed on the practice range where a more purposeful and target-oriented approach will help develop the habits that translate into game performance. It is there where the difference between *hitting balls* and *practicing shots* is realized, and it is there where the instinctive and intuitive aspects of one's game strengthens and greater trust in one's play builds.

51

Walking

Joined to the land,
the game is meant for walking—
and to do so fast.

I N 1995, THE United States Golf Association published a small booklet entitled *A Call to Feet: Golf Is a Walking Game.* The principal goal of the publication was "to reverse the inexcusable trend of riding in carts without a legitimate health concern." The publication identified several "problems" that golf carts have brought to the game, including asphalt cart paths scarring the golfing landscapes, gas carts fouling the atmosphere with their noxious fumes, the noise and movement of carts distracting players from their games, and the loss of caddy programs and the unique experience in sports that the companionship and guidance of a caddy provides during a round of golf.

The publication also addressed several "myths" about carts, including their effect on the pace of play (they do not necessarily ensure faster rounds); financial gain for a golf course (high maintenance fees and labor costs significantly undercut the profitability of a cart program); and economic necessity in order for a course to survive (which most courses in Ireland and Scotland and the increased number of "walking only" or preferred courses in the United States, like Bandon Dunes, Kiawah Island, Bethpage Black, Erin Hills, Whistling Straights, Pinehurst and Pebble Beach, refute).

But *A Call to Feet* is much more than an anti-cart manifesto. It is in fact an affirmation of the very essence of the game—human connection to a landscape. Its higher purpose is to celebrate that connection and to reveal how traversing a course seated on a cushion in a four-wheel vehicle bears no resemblance to engaging the game on two feet and enjoying its social dimensions with fellow walkers.

At a public course—in fact, a public *space*—like the grounds of the St. Andrews Links Trust, it is quite wonderful to recognize that those ancient seaside acres beckoned the use and enjoyment of the local community and visitors well before they became a sporting destination. Their transition to the latter reflected a choice that had as much to do with recreational promise as environmental appreciation and adaptation, and golf respected each of these factors. The insistence of the Links Trust that, with rare exception, its courses should be walked provides players with more than a spiritual connection to the six-hundred-year history of golf in this location. It affords a literal feel for the game and its pure elements. It promotes an understanding of how the land shaped the game and the game joined the land.

Moreover, as much as walking affirms the bond between the land and the game, it also enables a round to be played more quickly than "cart ball." This may seem counterintuitive to millions of golfers who have been riding in carts for most of their golfing lives or who have been playing courses that discourage walking either through their design or fee structure. Well beyond the aesthetic benefits absent the sights and sounds of fleets of golf carts racing and braking their way around a course while carrying their passengers, beer coolers, and massive bags, walking respects the rhythm of a round between shots, encourages shot readiness, and enables an appreciation for the quality and scenic beauty of courses. Walking champions the game as it was meant to be played—quickly paced, actively engaged, and truly shared. To recast Mark Twain's demeaning observation about the game, golf *with carts* is "a good walk spoiled" because the walk never occurred.

52

Partners

The journey offers
prospects of joy and reward—
choose your partners well.

T HE ESSENTIAL NATURE of golf's test is a lone individual confronting the demands of a course and striving to match par, the universal standard of performance. The endeavor conjures images of a solitary shepherd propelling some object with a stick over an ancient landscape toward a target. That first strike might have been taken out of boredom or curiosity, but at some point, and for whatever reason, he persisted. As his accuracy improved and he needed fewer strikes to hit the target, he must have told someone what he was doing among his flock out on the links land, and perhaps a contest ensued to determine who was more skilled at accomplishing the feat. At that moment, a single individual's amusement became social, and he found both a partner and a means to help transcend the existential loneliness of his being.

Sport provides a great variety of "partnerships" in the pursuit of common goals. Whether teammates number eleven or nine or five or even two, there is, of course, the basic matter of trying to succeed in the contest at hand. In working together, sporting partners not only have a chance to achieve victory, but they also can chip away at the walls that separate individuals from one another.

Here is where it really gets interesting. For sporting partners can find joy not only in sharing a game or a season with each other but also in accepting some responsibility for the kind of experience that their partners can have. True partners—in sport as in life—are persons who aim to make that experience as rewarding and enjoyable as it can possibly be for those who are joined with them in whatever the endeavor might be.

Golfing partners include teammates in a competitive event, whether that be a weekend better ball match at your home course or the battle of elite squads for a coveted trophy, such as the Ryder Cup or the national collegiate team championship. But just as certainly, and more routinely, playing partners are those who are simply paired in your group for the day's round. They are companions for the round. Whether these are people whom you know well or not at all, they are now joined with you in *play* and the task of enabling its enjoyment for all participants.

You can never tell what understanding in this regard your playing partners may have. You can hope that they are motivated to seek joy in the hours ahead, not suffering, but regardless of what they carry to the first tee, you can control your own attitude and effort. You can provide the right example and perhaps set the tone for the entire round for everyone. How mindful you are of your own temperament, how attentive and encouraging you are for your playing partners, how friendly and courteous your manner, how honest your play, how quick the pace of your game, how selfless your focus, how positive your karma—these are the habits of playing partners we all seek. Why not be the partner you want others to be?

Your other "partner" for the round is clearly the golf course itself. No matter their pedigree, rating, location, or reputation, courses convey their prospects as a promising partner through their appearance and the atmosphere it projects. Upkeep and conditioning are factors that signal respect and appreciation for anyone who has decided to play a round there, and they influence a decision to do so again. Yes, score matters and few would deny that the happiness of a 79 transcends the difference of one stroke from an 80; but just like the company of the players on a round, the look and feel of the course that hosts the round significantly affects the experience of the journey and how it will be remembered. Neglected grounds, shabby facilities, and unfriendly staff make it hard to conclude otherwise that a place is neither invested in your enjoyment nor interested in your return.

When play, company, and setting align, we are more likely to look back with satisfaction at the experience of good partners and a good round—no matter the score. That is a goal worth pursuing and, at the end of the day, a toast worth giving.

PAUL ZINGG

53

Solitude

In the cool grasses
a gallery of rabbits
for the lone player

A S THAT LONE ancient shepherd who first launched an object with his staff over the links land established, golf is essentially a solitary game. It compels the player to bring skill and nerve, memory and imagination to the task of meeting the challenges of the course and the day's conditions; and while the company of friends and playing partners highlights its social dimensions and appeal, they are not a requirement for a thoroughly enjoyable outing on a course. For this is a game where every shot is the player's own and playing alone gets to the heart of golf's nature—a game where a player is utterly alone in its conduct and consequences.

Yet there is so much more to playing alone than spiritual connection to the game's forebears. For the experience can be exhilarating, revealing, and liberating. It is, in other words, what you do with that solitude that makes it worthwhile; and like so much that is key to this game, *what* you do and *how* you do it is largely influenced by attitude and effort.

Playing alone on a course is very different from practicing alone on the range. For out on the course, your shots will be more purposeful than the range. You will more clearly gauge their results, and you are more likely to work on all aspects of your game. Perhaps most importantly, you are less likely to be obsessed with the mechanics of the swing once you give yourself "permission" to *play* the game rather than just pounding balls for hours without a whole lot of rhyme and reason. *Learn by doing* is not just an academic slogan.

Playing alone frees you from the foibles and distractions of playing partners—and their judgments about your game and the pressure they place on it. Assuming you start your round early in the morning or late in the afternoon when you are neither coming upon a group in front of you nor being pushed from behind, your pace of play and rhythm are your own, including the freedom to hit a second or third ball occasionally and to *play against the course*, not your fellow players.

Playing alone also frees your imagination not just regarding the shots to attempt but also the circumstances accompanying them. You can transport yourself and your game anywhere. You can be Carl Sprackler, Bill Murray's greenskeeper character in *Caddyshack*, imagining he is "an incredible Cinderella story" playing the final hole at Augusta with a one-shot lead. Adlibbing the entire scene, Murray blasts the heads off a row of flowers with a weeder, each swing producing a gloriously perfect shot on the way to victory in the Masters.

Or you can fire your imagination with a local scene on the course, such as that colony of rabbits that emerge from their warren late in the afternoon to graze in the rich tall grasses of the rough at the edge of the woods. Like a scene out of Richard Adams's delightful novel *Watership Down*, they gather for "silflay" in the fading light and cool air and watch you.[35] They are the least bit judgmental of your play, but you can imagine their quiet admiration and support for your efforts. They are your private gallery, which you acknowledge with a nod and a tip of your cap.

Such flights of fancy are most unlikely when playing in a group. Too bad. Golf is an all-too-human endeavor that a little humor and whimsy can only make more enjoyable.

54

Markers

A wish for the round,
benchmarks along the journey—
fairways and greens please.

" FAIRWAYS AND GREENS" has long been a wish for golfers as they embark on their rounds. Although a commonplace expression now, for most of the time of its usage, it was more the property of professional golfers, something like a secret password among an elite, knowing community. It held out the promise of *a good round* through the ability to hit fairways and gain greens in regulation. For these markers of a round's progress (like the number of putts taken or the percentage that a player successfully scrambles for a par or better when missing a green) provide some sense of a player's ability—and certainly satisfy the statisticians who crave ways to quantify the game and set comparative standards for proficiency in it.

Fairways and greens are not just benchmarks for a player's skill. They are among the most elemental design features of a golf course and central to the universal experience of the game. Whether it is the Extreme nineteenth hole at the Legend Golf Resort in South Africa, a hole that requires a helicopter to get to the tee perched on Hanglip Mountain 437 yards above the Africa-shaped green below, or the barely 100-yard long seventh hole at Pebble Beach, located at the tip of a peninsula surrounded by Monterey Bay, the goal is still the same—hit the green in one. Whether the fairway is 129 yards wide, as is the case for the shared first and eighteenth fairways of the Old Course at St. Andrews, or only 15 yards for the fourteenth at the Island Club north of Dublin, Ireland, the test is still the same—hit the fairway.

Although amassing fairways and greens in a round may translate into lower scores, such is not necessarily the case. Hitting fairways, although undoubtedly satisfying, may be greatly exaggerated in their importance in order to accomplish a fine score. Greens in regulation may correlate better to lower scores, but even tour professionals hit less than seven of ten greens on average in a competitive round.

Indeed, the notion of *a good round* itself has some universal markers related to score—for example, a par round or a personal best round regardless of score. This just underscores how subjective such a definition can be. When asked if a perfect round was 18 under par, Ben Hogan replied, "No, a perfect round would be 18." Unattainable perfection—even beyond the reach of Kim Jong-il, the former premier of North Korea. Seventeen bodyguards and the country's only golf pro have attested to witnessing the Dear Leader make five holes-in-one as he carded a 34 in his first round of golf at the par 72, 6,780-yard long Pyongyang Golf Course. Presumably, he saw no reason to try to top that, although it is rumored that he had eleven holes-in-one in a subsequent round.

Other notions of *a good round* are less quantifiable and fantastic—yet immeasurably satisfying and true. They focus on the notion—and the nature—of the journey. To complete a circuit of eighteen holes is to return home after daring to leave and facing many challenges to get back. It is to respect a game, one's playing partners, and, most of all, oneself through a journey that hinges on integrity and the possibility that something quite wonderful might occur during a round. It is to find a *fair way* in a *green* setting and to delight in knowing that someone has extended such a wish to you.

55

Greens

Fearing nor loathing
the speed and slope of the greens—
till the first three-putt

THERE IS NO aspect of playing the game that obsesses golfers more than putting. Evidence abounds to this effect. A glance at golf magazines or a search of the internet for information on game improvement will reveal an overwhelming focus of attention on putting than any other playing skill area. The golf equipment industry delights in reminding golfers that, since 35 percent to 45 percent of their strokes in a typical round will be taken with a putter, they need to choose this club wisely. Players from Willie Park and Young Tom Morris in the nineteenth century to the future members of the World Golf Hall of Fame who are now playing know that "a good player who is a great putter is a match for anyone; a great hitter who cannot putt is a match for no one."[36] Good putting, in other words, can hide a multitude of flaws elsewhere in a player's game, but bad putting will inevitably discount and frustrate good ball striking from tee to green.

Similarly, there is no aspect of a course that gets more attention or yields as much praise or scorn from players than the greens; and just as surely, no course will ever earn high regard without superior greens and green complexes. In fact, just the opposite is true. Even very ordinary layouts attract play and command respect if their greens are first rate.

There are many courses in Ireland and Scotland, for example, that are quite pedestrian, but they proudly proclaim that they have "the finest greens in the county" and attract a fair amount of play and good reviews because of the quality of their putting surfaces.

There are numerous factors that contribute to the quality and difficulty of greens. These begin with the location of the green, which is a significant aspect of the architect's vision for the entire course. Location includes the larger environment of the green complex, which takes into consideration such matters as bunkers and other greenside hazards, the length and contours of the hole, fairway access to the green, and other elements that make a hole fair, challenging, and interesting.

From there, the architect determines the size and shape of the green. All matters of slope, undulation, the type and height of the grass, and possible hole locations effect these decisions, but they all contribute to a fundamental recognition of the importance of play both on and around greens to test golfers of all abilities and the interdependence of green speeds and slopes.

If putting is the game's great equalizer, fast greens are where the great putters stand out from the pack; but there are some putting surfaces that can confound—if not, terrorize—all players. Certain greens that call to mind Sam Snead's confession about what he most feared in golf: "Lightning, Ben Hogan, and downhill putts."

These are places such as Augusta National, Pine Valley, and the golf course at Yale University where massive undulations characterize the greens and green speeds significantly exceed that which their architects originally imagined. Pinehurst No. 2 where the Donald Ross-designed convex putting surfaces, false fronts of greens, and variety of perilous hole locations near the edges of greens conspire not just to make three-putts a routine possibility but also an achievement. Royal Melbourne, Royal Dornoch, and Old Macdonald at Bandon Dunes where the strong winds that can sweep over these links play havoc with any ball rolling across their raised, wavy putting areas. Oakmont where the green speeds are actually slowed down a bit from their normal 14 to 15 on the Stimpmeter for events like the U.S. Open.[37] Prairie Dunes where the ubiquitous ridges, depressions, spines, and mounds on the greens have been labeled "Maxwell Rolls" after the course's designer, Maxwell Perry. And the Old Course at St. Andrews where it seems that every green—from the relatively round and flat ninth to the monstrous, nearly-one-acre putting surface shared by the fifth and thirteenth holes—offers diversity, difficulty, memorability, and awe.

"Putting greens," said Charles Blair Macdonald, a fine amateur player, aggressive patron of American golf, and the designer of such wonderful courses as the National Golf Links, Chicago Golf Club, and the original Lido Golf Club, "are to golf courses what faces are to portraits." Yes, every portrait needs a face, and every golf course greens. But just as there is a vast difference between Leonardo's *Mona Lisa* (1503) and Picasso's *Seated Woman* (1937), although both are portraits of seated women, the world of golf encompasses a great variety of greens and green complexes.

The subject matter of greens, of course, is the same—an area of closely trimmed grass that allows a player to complete a hole with the precision that is required to stroke a ball into the cup, but their expressions on grass can be as classic or conceptual as any artist can produce on canvas. So too the responses they evoke from homage to horror.

56

Rules

The ball as it lies
and the course as you find it—
defining the game.

T HE *RULES OF Golf*—whether those first announced by the Gentlemen Golfers of Leith on March 7, 1744, or any of their subsequent iterations by the Royal and Ancient Golf Club of St. Andrews and the United States Golf Association—flow from two basic working principles, one fundamental purpose, and a mighty caveat.

The *principles* are stated in this *haiku:* To play the course as the golfers find it and to play the ball as it lies. Their *purpose*: To ensure that everyone plays by the same rules. The *caveat*: If you can't play the course as you find it or the ball as it lies, then play *fair*. This caveat has a caveat: in order to do what is fair, know the *Rules of Golf.*

This secondary caveat sounds a lot like Ben Hogan's advice to young Nick Faldo when the latter asked him how he could win tournaments. Said Hogan, "Shoot lower scores."

If only it were that simple. The official rule book of the USGA is over two hundred pages long, and it is constantly in flux as it deals with new situations affecting how the game is played. Examples include ball and equipment changes, efforts to speed up the pace of play, and factors affecting how it is governed. Regarding the latter, a new rule going into effect in 2018 states that tournament officials will no longer consider call-ins by television and internet viewers on alleged rules infractions. To be sure, this is a matter that the gentlemen golfers of the eighteenth century did not give much thought.

But *fairness* did command their attention, and it remains the heart of the matter because the rules do not just govern the conduct of play. They also define the character of the game.

Such was the case within those original thirteen rules for the game upon the links land of East Lothian. They emphasized that a ball is put in play at the start of a hole and that it is not touched again until the ball has been holed and lifted from the cup. Moreover, and governing the entire set of rules, was the explicit directive that this pursuit should be undertaken *honestly* and not causing interference with the play of others.[38]

Although breaches of etiquette in the conduct of the game, such as dishonest handicaps, discourteous play, or behavior that injures or otherwise contributes to the detriment of the game's enjoyment by others are neither covered by the rules *per se* nor necessarily incur penalty strokes, they can invite disciplinary action. In fact, the governing bodies for the game encourage that this be the case and that response can be harsh, including disqualification from an event and withdrawal of playing privileges from a club, a course, or a tournament. As the USGA and the R&A state, such actions are "considered to be justifiable in terms of protecting the interests of the majority of golfers who wish to play in accordance with these guidelines."[39]

There is a reason for all of this. Etiquette is an integral part of the game, for it fairly defines the game's core values, which include sportsmanship, civility, and courtesy, but none more fundamental than respect—for the course, for fellow players, for the game. Its demonstration affirms a commitment to the integrity of the game and marks the character of those who play it.

Greater perhaps than any other sport, how a golfer conducts himself or herself constitutes a *moral* imperative. For the very definition of morality is "right rules of conduct." Golf's right rules are grounded not within a list of dos and don'ts or homage to some arcane pastime of the privileged but in an affirmation of the spirit of the game and an invitation to anyone who plays it—regardless of age, gender, handicap, social standing, or financial circumstances—to honor it.

The rules invite players to *play away* and *play fair*. Not a bad bottom line.

57

Wayward

In a toad's manner
the ball hops across the path—
the sound of silence

AS SPORTS PSYCHOLOGIST Bob Rotella emphasizes, "golf is not a game of perfect." Moreover, as he and so many teachers and accomplished players understand, it is a game where managing one's imperfect shots and efforts is one of the vital keys to achieving success in the game. Says Hall of Famer Annika Sorenstam: "Golf is not just a game of great shots. It's a game of bad shots, too. The champions are the ones who hit the fewest bad shots and who are smart enough to keep their bad shots from being terrible."[40]

Sorenstam's fierce determination and rigorous approach to the game brought her unparalleled success. Throughout the course of her fourteen-year professional career, she won ninety tournaments worldwide, including ten Majors. She was eight times the player of the year on the Ladies Professional Golf Association tour. Her perspective on the nature of the game—and its humbling reality for even the greatest players—may be the strongest lesson she learned as a player and has since imparted.

Yet also consider the wisdom gained on the occasion of a wayward shot from a very different source—Sammy Cahn and Jimmy Van Heusen's composition "Straight Down the Middle." Written for Bing Crosby, who recorded its most famous version in 1957, the song became the anthem for Crosby's annual tournament at Pebble Beach (now the AT&T National Pro-Am), if not for golfer's everywhere. Here is its first stanza:

> Straight down the middle
> It went straight down the middle
> Then it started to hook just a wee bit
> That's when my caddie lost sight of it
> That little white pellet has never been found to this day
> But it went straight down the middle far away

In a single shot—joy, satisfaction, distress, despair, resignation, hope. In other words, life; and like life, what comes next?

Like Sorenstam and Rotella, in fact, preceding them and undoubtedly influencing them, the man who pursued perfection like no other—Ben Hogan—had his own spin on its quest. "Golf is a game of misses," Hogan agreed. But then added: "The guy who *misses the best* is going to win."

Hogan turned the brutal nature of the game on its head and made its encounter a strength. What Hogan brought to his game was not only thorough ownership of his swing but also intense focus and purpose for every shot he took. Those shots were informed by keen self-awareness of his playing skills, tendencies, and capacities and his ability to visualize their application on the course he was playing. His process of visualizing success included a balance between taking risks and employing caution and knowing where and how to recover from a poor shot in order to save par or at least eliminate a big number.

This is the essence of course management—to play the right shot at the right time that takes into account the circumstances of the immediate moment and the goal of achieving the best possible score for the round.

That goal, of course, will vary significantly depending upon a player's skill level, but bringing strategic *thinking* to a round is something that any player can do. For no matter what a player's skill level may be, a successful round is closely tied to the attitude and plan that a player brings to the first tee.

And of course, to have the discipline to sustain a positive outlook and approach throughout the round. Yes, poor shots and mistakes will occur. After all, this is golf. But what allows a player to recover from a bad shot and not be defeated in silent resignation to misfortune? Look inward, said Arnold Palmer, look at what a golfer can control—attitude and effort. Or more bluntly from the king: "If you're stupid enough to whiff, you should be smart enough to forget it!"

58

Winter

On a day like this,
no ball marks on frozen greens—
no wait on first tee

THE SIGHT OF the winter's first snow covering the ground is a startling reminder that golf is an outdoors game. For millions of devoted golfers who do not live where more temperate climes support play year round, the elements of the coldest months raise two main prospects for tending to one's game while the sleet falls and the greens freeze—hibernate or vacate. The former takes players to a passive season of *watching*—viewing the game being televised from distant warm venues and standing in front of mirrors straining to translate into muscle memory the images of perfection that the golf magazines and videos proffer. The latter tempts the fortunate few to find a welcome, however brief, respite from winter's conditions through golf-oriented escapes to various deserts, islands, or southern beaches. In an annual migration, the "snow birds" from Canada descend on Myrtle Beach, and the Baja Peninsula swarms with visitors in search of tequila shots and birdie putts.

Yet even in the middle of the cold, upon the frost-withered fairways and under the bare tree branches, the game cannot be denied. Every course has a hearty band of players who will answer its siren call no matter what the weather conditions, but the game does have its requirements for enjoyment when the temperatures plummet and the north winds blow. Foremost among these are preparation and perspective.

Dressing properly should be obvious, but certain tips are worth heeding. Since our body will lose most of its heat through the head and hands, it is vital to keep them covered. The value of a ski cap and mittens cannot be overstated. Carrying a hand warmer is a good idea as well. The key for the entire body is layering and to choose the right, lightweight clothing fabrics that will allow adding or reducing layers for maximum comfort and swing movement. Your friendly pro shop and nearby golf retailer will happily provide all that you need.

What goes in your body is as important as what covers it. The goal is to boost the body's metabolism through high-protein food and beverages that stimulate the nervous system and get the body to work harder and to avoid intake that will lower body temperature. Hydration is vitally important but alcohol of any sort needs to wait until the round is over. The hot toddy in the clubhouse after such a round will never taste so good.

This kind of preparation is actually the easy part. It's the mental game—*isn't it always?*—that ultimately makes winter golf possible and enjoyable. In brief, adjust expectations. The conditions are such that shooting a career round is most unlikely. In fact, more modest expectations can actually have a liberating effect on one's game. For unburdened of the self-imposed pressure of achieving a particular score, what is left is what is most basic—a willingness to accept and engage the challenges of the conditions, the delight of company who will do this with you, and the sights and wonders of how a brisk, snowy day has transformed familiar golfing grounds into a winter landscape. Listen especially to the very different sounds that such days yield as a round progresses. Heed the sounds of stillness.

No, you do not need to pack your clubs away for the winter or bring them out only for a trip to the tropics. Nor do you need slow play, a backup on the par 3s, long lines at the snack bar, and high anxiety accompanying you to the first tee—any time. To be sure, winter golf has its own special challenges and scenarios, but its unique joys include the chance to discover and rediscover some of the most compelling attractions of the game. For that reason alone, dress warmly, bring a yellow ball to the first tee, embrace the punch shot, salute the brave company who are out there with you—and *carpe diem!*

59

Renewal

Spring air and soft days,
clubs undust and swings unwind—
this will be the year!

WINTER IS THE cruelest of seasons for golfers. The summer sunshine and high skies that accompanied our rounds only a few months earlier have faded from memory. Short days and snow clouds have replaced them. We are in a holding pattern that seems to get longer with every passing year. The game is never that far away, though, but it seems more rumor than reality in the calendar's twilight.

The December holiday season arrives with the latest in golf-related gifts. A coffee table book filled with beckoning images of the world's greatest courses. The hottest instructional video offering the final key to unlocking the potential of one's game. It will be added to the box in the basement where eight-track tapes, cassettes, and CDs of similar promises have been accumulating for years. There might even be the newest product from the Marquis de Sade golf laboratories—some whip, strap, brace, or weight that seems more appropriate as a medieval instrument of torture than a golf aid. And perhaps a new driver or putter—its design features lovingly admired and its playing capabilities brilliantly imagined.

January brings television broadcasts from the first tour events of the New Year in Hawaii. Inevitably, at some point during the coverage, the cameras will pan over the impossibly blue ocean and perfect beaches adorned with bikini-clad sunbathers, and an announcer will say something like "We hope that these images of paradise will bring some cheer to those back east who are suffering from the coldest winter on record." It doesn't.

Although the shortest month, February seems interminably long. The PGA tour has moved on to Arizona and southern California, and the golf magazines are helping readers ready their games and shape their bodies for the spring. More importantly, a brave crocus pushes its way up from the earth, and an icicle melts in the slanted sun of days slowly growing longer. A late storm will no doubt descend, its numbing cold a bitter check on the anticipation of winter's ending. But there's enough certainty in spring's arrival that clubs will move from the garage to the trunk of the car, and a trip to the range will test the new driver.

It has been said that February lasts only as long as it takes to get to March, but it is the month when winter begins to slip away, leaving March with the official task of proclaiming its departure. Yet even after the vernal equinox, some remnants of winter may linger. The wildflowers and warmth of March, however, are not the accidents that they seemed to be in February.

Similarly, the golf commentators and magazines are discussing the Masters in the present tense, and nothing in the world of golf announces the arrival of spring more certainly than the azaleas in bloom at Augusta. Like everything else that begins again in the spring, the state of a golfer's game and the hopes accompanying it are renewed. For just as every baseball team has a chance for the post-season in spring training, every golfer imagines that *this could be the year!*

60

Yearning

Old legs and dim eyes
strain for the fairways and greens
of a distant round.

T HERE IS SIMPLY no avoiding it—we are all getting older. Although we may not spend a lot of time contemplating this fact of life in our youth, the evidence clearly confronts us by the time we reach our thirties and forties.

Several of the changes in our body that are occurring by then particularly affect golfers, as they do all athletes. Like the great majority of humans, we will see our metabolism, that is, our body's ability to digest and process food slow. This has obvious implications for weight gain and the aches and pains that come with additional stress on our legs, backs, and hearts. It also contributes, slowly but surely, unless arrested with dietary changes and exercise, to a decline in the percentage of our muscle mass, which will naturally drop about 1 percent a year after age twenty-five. As we lose muscle mass, we lose stamina and flexibility, making it harder to warm up for a round and sustain its demands on our body through eighteen holes. To add insult to injury, we may experience increased difficulty actually seeing these changes because of presbyopia, a form of vision loss that begins around age forty and affects more than a billion people in the world.

Although the aging process is inevitable, it can, in fact, be slowed—or at least—and entire industries have arisen to accomplish this. Offering prescriptions and products that range in inspiration from the Fountain of Youth to Dorian Gray, they promise fitness, happiness, beauty, and success.

The golf industry is no exception to this phenomenon, especially with its focus on a particular malady facing aging golfers—loss of distance. The annual arrival of new golf equipment increasingly reflects the demands of a graying golfing population with balls, club heads, shafts, driver lofts, club construction materials, and even tees all promising to generate more distance for golfers with lower swing speeds and less power at impact. Videos, seminars, and publications focus on tips and programs aimed at developing greater strength and flexibility in order to help golfers turn back the clock and maximize how far they can hit the ball.

There are, of course, more keys to success and happiness in this game for older golfers than the latest equipment and fitness routines, shorter courses, and modified expectations—or memories of career rounds and glory days long ago. This gets to the heart of the matter of this *haiku*. This is the mind-set that senior players bring to their games.

The mind of a golfer, like anyone, tends to visit the past or go to the future. A solid driving round one day may recall those rounds and days when this was commonplace, and even though the drive today may seldom travel two hundred yards, the fact that it is well struck is enough to imagine that the halcyon days of drives considerably longer can return. The past and the future become the focus when in fact it is the present that is reality and should command attention.

Reorienting one's mind to this awareness is not to concede defeat to the aging process. To be sure, fitness programs, dietary changes, modern equipment, improving accuracy off the tee, and working on the short game can help seniors achieve low scores. Ultimately, it is *attitude and effort*—things we can control—that can be brought to the reality of getting older and which will make the greatest difference in one's game.

Being *in the moment* is as much an acceptance of where we are as it is an affirmation to make the most of how we are. Distance off the tee is not everything. As Harvey Penick, the author of *Harvey Penick's Little Red Book*, the highest selling golf book ever, reminds us, "The woods are full of long drivers." But *going the distance*, continuing to find happiness and companionship through this great game for an entire lifetime, is a lot closer to what truly matters.

61

Remains

Why do we keep them,
the scorecards that log our rounds?
where have we put them?

G OLF IS DEEPLY rooted in description and story and rewards those who *read* the game well. There may be no other game that provides as much to read or encourages such close reading in order to comprehend its appeal and succeed with its challenges. The rich literature of the game—represented in the seminal writings of Bernard Darwin, Charles Blair Macdonald, Alister Mackenzie, Joyce Wethered, and Herbert Warren Wind and the instructional classics of Byron Nelson, Ben Hogan, Dave Pelz, Jack Nicklaus, and Harvey Penick—is only one expression of the reading that the game offers. Course guides and yardage books are others as their numbers, symbols, illustrations, and commentary introduce the fields of play. The rule book provides a deeper read of a different kind. It defines the conduct of the game and, in the closeness of its study and practice, the character of the player.

The knowledge that flows from these sources, though, receives its fullest meaning within the context of personal experience. Whether in the moment or through the passage of time, there is no more personal chronicle of one's engagement with this game than the scorecard. For here in stark markings is evidence of how well a player has absorbed the many narratives that provide insight, inspiration, and information to appreciate this game and improve one's play.

But more fundamentally, the scorecard reveals the ability of a player to recall the stories of his own experience and apply them to the situations he encounters in a round. Advice and technique for "reading" a green or the lie of a ball in a bunker—among a myriad of examples—abound, but the key is the translation of that knowledge through experience into performance. Like *haiku,* the success of the translation depends upon the authenticity of the narrative and the integrity of the read.

What do we remember about a particular shot in a similar situation? Which narratives among the countless we have stored in our head do we choose to recall? Is the experience of our memory true? *How* we read is as important as *what* we read, for the actions we take are informed by both the perspectives we bring to the reading and the circumstances accompanying it.

The scorecard also serves as a bridge between the transient moments of a round and the enduring narrative of a player's history with the game. We save scorecards for many reasons—evidence of progress on a golfing bucket list, a round of particular achievement with a hole-in-one or personal best score, a day and a place shared with special company, an item in the scrapbook or diary of a long anticipated trip, a celebrity's autograph. Some may get framed and appear on a desk or a wall for a while, but most will end up in a box in the garage and never see the light of day again.

The remains of a round most worth saving, though, are those that transcend the fleeting moments of accomplishment or futility, which the marks on a scorecard record. How we approach a round will influence what we take away from it. For every round affords the opportunity to strengthen not only our performance in the game but also our understanding of why this game matters. Surely, these are outcomes more likely achieved with an open and hopeful attitude than bringing dread, disinterest, and sufferance to the task. When we embrace the former, the "scorecards" we are more likely to keep and value have a lot less to do with writing down numbers than tolling the reasons why we treasure this game.

62

Waiting

Waiting out the storm,
wordlessly watching the sky,
willing the brightness

THE LONG ANTICIPATED round or golfing trip has arrived. All matters of travel, reservations, and scheduling have been addressed. The first tee time calls, but you are not on the tee box. Instead, you are huddled with your playing companions under the eaves of the starter's hut or anxiously peering through the windows of the clubhouse as a deluge of biblical proportions descends on the course and threatens to wash away your plans.

For days—if not months—you have obsessively been checking out various weather apps and reports, scanning the forecasts, and studying the trends. It is a process that has led you to surf among them to find the one with the most promising weather news or even a tiny crack in the dismal scene now confronting you. Despite your best efforts to avoid or prepare for it, you are now confounded by the one factor you cannot control—bad weather.

Yes, the golfing specials at Bandon Dunes and Cabot Links are truly spectacular in November, but so too are the prewinter storms that can rage across those wonderful grounds. Access to the Old Course is hardly a problem in February, if you don't mind playing off a pad of artificial turf, which players are encouraged to use, or cover every inch of your body with Everest-ready layers of clothing, hats, and gloves. Whether it is the hurricanes of August and September along the Carolina coasts, midsummer thunder storms in the midwest and northeast, or something more ferocious than the "soft" days in Ireland, weather can wreak havoc on the best-laid plans for a golf game.

Not surprising—because the Emerald Isle is green for good reason— Ireland has developed a unique vocabulary to deal with the 150 to 200 days of rain that parts of the country experience annually.[41] This ranges from "spitting" and "wetting" conditions to monstrous days of "hooring," "lashing," and "hammering." The gentle end of the rain scale permits most outdoor activities. The horrid end goes well beyond such conventional descriptions as "rotten" or "raining buckets." This is rain that even the Irish speak about in hushed tones with warnings not to tempt ruin by venturing out.

Yet golfers will.

Often the motivation is the time and investment that brought them to a particular place at a particular time. There's no going back, no refunds, no rain checks. If this is a once-in-a-lifetime experience, the disappointment may be so overwhelming that only two options appear to be the case—rail against the conditions and the ill-fortune that brought them or deal, however grudgingly, with the situation. Neither approach is necessarily filled with a lot of joy.

But there is a third choice. It is well to remember that golf originated on coarse and obdurate grounds and was regularly pursued through such challenging weather conditions as low temperatures, high winds, and steady rains. Indeed, the Scottish expression "Nae wind, nae rain, nae golf" says it all.

Channeling one's inner Scotsman, especially a nineteenth-century gentleman dressed in heavy woolens and pounding a featherie across scruffy links land, is not the stuff of ordinary pleasure for most contemporary golfers, but those were hearty pioneers of a vexing game back then. An occasional connection to them through testing one's ability—and *attitude*—in dire conditions can be as much a spiritual exercise as a means to a deeper appreciation of both the origins of the game and its evolution. Imagine the tales that can be told and the bonds that are formed by completing eighteen holes in the foulest weather. Consider the delight of your fellow golfers when you raise a toast at round's end to Willie Park Sr. for capturing his second Open at Prestwick in 1863 in dreadful conditions similar to what you may have just experienced.

Is play in such conditions better than no golf at all? It is safe to say at least sometimes. But equipped with a sense of humor and history and a wee bit of courage, *why not?*

63

Rain

Round interrupted,
bemoaning the rain's fury—
and no umbrella

A T ONE TIME or another, it has happened to all golfers. The much-anticipated round, whether a special trip or just the regular Saturday fourball after a long workweek, threatened by rain. But optimism, however cautious, endures. Perhaps the *Weather Channel* is wrong, and all those deep green and yellow radar images of gathering rain clouds are just an illusion. Perhaps the dry ground, after the long drought, will absorb the impending deluge, and the course will be playable. Perhaps the solid dark gray clouds above, accompanied with ominous thunder rolls, will break up, and pockets of brightness will appear. Perhaps this is just a roiling squib rushing through or the tolerable conditions of an Irish "soft day."

Perhaps. Or perhaps it's the end of the world—or at least the end of the day's golfing plans.

And perhaps it's just weather. Refreshing, bracing weather that moved the Victorian Age art critic John Ruskin to write that "there is really no such thing as bad weather, only different kinds of good weather."

Well, tell that to Tiger Woods whose quest for the modern grand slam was derailed by weather in the third round of the Open at Muirfield in 2002. After earlier victories that year at the Masters and the U.S. Open, Woods suffered an 81 in the black Scottish twilight of gusting forty-mile-per hour winds and torrential rains off the North Sea. The score was the highest he had ever posted as a professional to that time, and it punctuated the opinion of his fellow players that the weather conditions that day were the most wretched in the history of the Open.

But also share Ruskin's observation with Tom Kite, who won the United States Open at Pebble Beach in 1992 in similarly horrid conditions that produced a final round scoring average of 77.3, the third highest in the post-World War II Open era. Said Kite about his even par 72, which was accomplished during the worst hours of the harsh weather: "When I woke up Sunday morning at the Open and stepped outside and felt the wind and rain in my face, I knew I had an excellent chance to win if I just took my time and trusted myself."

Sometimes, wrote the American poet Henry Wadsworth Longfellow, "the best I think that one can do about the rain is to let it rain." This Zen-like observation is not quite a call to become "one with the rain," but it counsels a response to harsh weather that is neither defeatist nor dispassionate. It is a recognition that here is a challenging condition that all the players, more or less, depending upon the luck of tee times and the movement of storm systems, will face this day. Some will do so reluctantly, even angrily. Some will smell the rain, feel the wind, and embrace the challenge more positively, yet there is no guarantee that the latter approach will necessarily yield a better score than the former.

There is, though, a much better chance that those who embrace the test of tough weather conditions—rather than those who simply shout at them—will come away from the experience better connected to the game and the reasons why they play it. Just as the game defies perfection, there are those days with far-less-than-perfect conditions to undertake a round. Yet even on such occasions, there is still the opportunity to reveal the character of both the game and those who play it. There can be laugh-out-loud exhilaration trying to hit a shot in the teeth of a gale-force wind. Or sorry damnation of how unfair the conditions are. With whom would you prefer to play a round? And what example of playing in these elements will you provide?

Yes, into every life some rain will fall. And yes, as much as golfers jokingly try to reassure each other as they drive through the downpours on the way to the club, it does, indeed, rain on a golf course. And sometimes very hard. A chance to excel, as Tom Watson would have it. And a chance for the real golfers to identify themselves.

64

Practice

Thunder clouds move in,
no one on the practice range—
except Hogan's ghost.

" IF I MISS one day of practice," said the great Polish pianist Ignacy Jan Paderewski, "I notice it. If I miss two days, the critics notice it. If I miss three, the audience notices it."

Paderewski's self-awareness and high personal standard of excellence directly flowed from his work ethic. He studied his music and instrument with relentless dedication, and no less than his stage presence, that commitment underscored his piano virtuosity and popular appeal. So renowned his accomplishments, it was not unusual for critics to say of his protégés and rivals that, yes, they played well, "but they were no Paderewesky." For Paderewsky *owned* his music.

Few golfers have owned their games in the same fashion. Harry Vardon, Bobby Jones, Ben Hogan, Arnold Palmer, Jack Nicklaus, Annika Sorenstam, Tom Watson, Tiger Woods. The list is not very long, and the names on it reflect very different styles and games, but one common denominator—they embraced practice. They saw their time on the range or in the shop not as a form of puritanical penance for the joy they found in playing their game but as a pathway to self-discovery and satisfaction in knowing that they did their best to play their best.

Hogan's work ethic was the most driven, even demonic in its intensity. Often practicing twelve hours a day, his explanation was simple: "Every day you miss playing or practicing is one day longer it takes to be good." Few of his fellow players or anyone appreciated how such traumatic experiences in his life as childhood poverty, his father's suicide, and a near-fatal car crash or his efforts to "game" his competition drove his constant focus on perfection. "Out work 'em. Out think 'em. Then you intimidate 'em" was his simple formula for tournament success, and that is how he defined his life. Warding off close friends and even denying having children were conscious decisions to avoid distraction from what he was so obsessed to accomplish. And practice—constant, hard, bloodied hand practice—was a means to those goals.

He was mesmerizing to watch. The ball just sounded different leaving his club, and he seemed to forge his own tracks in the sky. No one matched the respect he earned through the way he worked at his game, but Hogan's way was not the only way. Just when his hard-edged focus seemed the necessary road to greatness, along came Arnold Palmer, and both the work and play of golf made a welcome turn to a more broadly accessible and appealing place.

To be sure, Palmer fully embraced the hard work of perfecting his game, an ethos that he learned from his father. He recognized quite early in his career that "the harder you practice, the luckier you get." But unlike Hogan, who discovered as much about his game "in the dirt" of practice as he found pleasure in its isolation, Palmer thoroughly enjoyed pounding balls, working their flight, and experimenting with clubs. Well into his eighties, Palmer either hit balls or tinkered in his workshop nearly every day of his life. He did this because he *chose* to do so, not because he felt he *had* to do so.

Palmer's love of the game was infectious. It attracted legions of loyal fans to him personally and to the game, and he returned their affection enthusiastically and generously, a far cry from the reclusive, secretive Hogan and the cold quality of his craftsmanship. Golf's popular boom in the 1960s was spurred by Palmer's triumphs and charisma, not because he was the "anti-Hogan" but because he played the game with such obvious joy and passion. He was golf's Everyman to Hogan's Superman, a hero with a human touch, neither remote nor inscrutable.

But Hogan and Palmer—and every player seeking success in the game—knew that practice was part of the game. It has been said that there is no glory in practice, but without practice there is no glory. Even more basically, there is little prospect for finding one's place in the game—however lofty or grounded that might be—without working on one's game in a deliberate and purposeful manner. The outcome might not be perfection despite its occasional glimpses—or the illusion thereof. It can be greater satisfaction in how the game is played and, even more so, fuller appreciation for why.

65

Wonder

Wind's test at land's end,
a flip wedge a full hybrid—
seven at Pebble.

AFTER A RELATIVELY benign opening five holes, where the sea is more a rumor than a factor, first-time players may question what is so special about this place, but then the long climb up the rising fairway of the par 5 sixth provides at last a sense of the setting and the demands of the course that awaits. It is a walk that reveals how the Pebble Beach Golf Links is less a links course than a headlands layout with its spectacular view of Stillwater Cove about sixty feet below the sheer cliffs bordering the entire right side of the hole. What newcomers do not realize is that this is the easiest of the ocean holes ahead, and it offers no hint whatsoever about what lies just over the crest of the green.

For what awaits at seven is so much more than one of the most thrilling and perplexing holes in all of golf.

Its physical features are easy to describe. The hole measures barely one hundred yards long, making it the shortest hole on any of the courses where golf's Major championships are held. Resting about twenty feet below a tiny plateau tee is a somewhat heart-shaped speck of green. It is surrounded by a necklace of shallow bunkers and perched only a few steps from the exposed rocks and breaking waves of the Pacific Ocean.

Behind the tee, below and to the right, and ahead beyond the green is Monterey Bay.

Yet this grand ensemble of location and design makes the playing characteristics of this hole almost impossible to explain. For how to explain a hole that requires a three-quarter wedge one day and a strong four-iron the next? A hole that has been played with serious intent with both a putter and a driver off the tee. A short par 3 that has yielded aces to the highest handicap amateurs and quadruple bogies to the best professionals. A green that is so close to the tee that it seems you can just reach out and touch it, and then again, its placement only guessed when the spray of the roiling surf and shrouds of storm-borne rain and fog cover it and engulf you.

Like no other hole at Pebble, and few anywhere, the seventh also reveals how the elements of surprise and anticipation are deeply rooted in golf. Whether one has played this hole a hundred times or for the first time, players know that it is coming—players want it to come—even though it is not even seen until one arrives at the tee. This feeds a sense of hopeful expectation that accompanies something that one looks forward to doing, and when this sense is joined with a receptivity to being surprised—even to being caught unawares—it opens up grand possibilities for discovery and delight.

Surprise and anticipation have both passive and active dimensions to them. The former occurs on this site through the sensorial intensity of the setting—crashing waves, roaring surf, barking seals, endless views, splendid isolation. It is a privilege to be here. The latter summons the memories of our golfing experiences and the evidence within them to believe that *this green* can be hit and *this par* can be made. Standing on the tee at seven at Pebble transcends space and summons the prospects of what might be. It is a place of beauty, hope, and wonder. It is all that a great golf hole should be.

PAUL ZINGG

66

Golf Gods

Ball struck long and true,
unfound and unaccounted—
the gods must have it.

UPON WINNING THE 2001 Masters, Tiger Woods explained: "Some of the golfing gods are looking down on me the right way."

Contemplating golf's ultimate reward, a hole-in-one, Charlie Brown of cartoon *Peanuts* fame says to his avid golf-playing dog, Snoopy, "I find it strange that the golf gods have never allowed you to have a hole-in-one. I wonder what that means."

To which Snoopy replies, "It means we need some new golfing gods."

As his creator, Charles Schulz, a lifelong golfer who did not accomplish a hole-in-one until age seventy-three, understood, the influence of the golfing gods is a vexing matter. How can solid single-digit handicappers go through their entire golfing lives without one, while others who can barely break 100 have sometimes experienced more than one? Is the answer beyond mortal performance or explanation?

Who then might the golf gods be? Are they implorable deities with form and name? Are they shapeless spirits, a life force that both animates and mystifies the game? Or perhaps they are mere chimeras amusingly and conveniently conjured up to provide some explanation for good fortune and not during a round.

In whatever manner of appearance or presence, what do they do? Are they fair arbiters of all things about the game? Or are they a tribunal of bodiless hackers who aim to impose their pitiful games on the living? Or are they simply a reminder that we control a lot less than we care to admit about a game we seek to master?

The answers to these questions are deeply rooted in the fascination that men and women throughout history have had with forces and beings allegedly possessed of supernatural powers and attributes and which seem to find no human affair unworthy of their attention or irresistible of their influence. These are beings as eager to torment and beguile as to favor and protect, as interested in victory and defeat on a grand scale as human drama on its most intimate levels. With equal relish and mischief, they observe and effect human behavior on battlefields and in bedrooms.

If nothing is too great or inconsequential to merit the attention of such beings, then why not a game and its pursuit? And why not a game where good and evil, temptation and revelation, godly moments and god-awful ones, blend together so seamlessly? Could the gods resist such a toy?

Observations about the interactions between the human and the divine have engaged poets and philosophers, theologians and teachers for several millennia. From Thales of Miletus in the seventh century BC ("All things are full of gods") to John Lennon in the twentieth century AD ("I believe that what people call God is something in all of us"), they provide a framework to consider the presence and influence of the golf gods. Or more precisely, the forces and spirits that move golfers to pursue their game and reconcile their efforts.

Whether they exist as articles of faith or inventions of whimsy, the golf gods find their basis for existence in golf's unique blend of skill and science and chance that makes the game so inscrutable and seductive. It is not unlike the appeal of trying to fathom the unknowable—the very essence of God.

67

Slow Play

A bale of turtles
moving at a glacial pace—
or sloth of golfers?

F ROM THE UNITED States Golf Association to the local muni, from individuals who are leaving the game to those who worry about how to sustain it, there is a common refrain—*a round of golf takes far too long to play.* Even more so than the high costs of rounds and equipment and the discouraging length of time it takes to develop a satisfactory level of proficiency in the game, slow play is the bane of the sport. It strains friendships, ruins rounds, fuels exasperation, and turns a much anticipated golfing outing into a dispirited day where focus and pleasure are the first casualties.

But it's even more serious than this. Both the USGA and the National Golf Foundation have concluded that slow play is a primary reason for a steady decline in the popularity of golf. Some of the evidence to this effect is a 10:1 ratio of course closings to openings over the past decade, a corresponding decrease in rounds played annually over the same period, and surveys of golfers revealing their concerns about the health and appeal of the game.

Both the USGA and the Royal and Ancient Golf Club have proposed a series of rules changes for implementation in 2019 designed to speed up play, such as reducing the time allotted to search for a lost ball, simplifying ball drop and hazard play options, and encouraging a "hit-when-ready" pace. This action follows two earlier USGA campaigns to address slow play. The first, *A Call to Feet: Golf Is a Walking Game*, debuted in 1995 and addressed not only the aesthetic and health benefits of walking a course but also the myth that riding in carts was necessarily a faster way to complete a round than walking.

A more recent campaign launched in 2013 specifically addressed slow play. In a series of thirty-second infomercials featuring Arnold Palmer, Annika Sorenstam, Tiger Woods, Paula Creamer, Butch Harmon, and Clint Eastwood, the USGA humorously played off the line "While we're young" from the film *Caddyshack* to encourage a swifter pace of play.

Unfortunately, there is scant evidence to suggest that any of these efforts have had a positive impact on the time it takes to play a round. We are still faced with familiar questions and scenarios. Why is it that foursomes are held up by threesomes . . . who are held up by twosomes? How many angles are necessary to examine a two-foot putt? Is it that hard to be "shot ready" by checking your yardages or reading your putting line *before* it is your turn to play? Can we not agree to play "ready golf" when your group is falling behind the one in front of you? Seriously, how many practice swings are necessary? How close are you to the "twenty second" guideline that the USGA suggests is the approximate time it should take to hit a shot once you approach your ball? Why do players not choose to play from tees that are more appropriate for their handicaps or how far they hit the ball? And why is it that slow players never think that *they* are slow?

To be sure, courses can influence the pace of play through the way a course is conditioned and set up, guidelines for which tees to play, marshalling, and overall encouragements both aggressive and subtle to pick up the pace of play. And just as certainly, it is *not just other golfers* who are at fault for slow play.

The efforts that have the best chance to speed up the pace of play, though, are those where courses and clubs try to create a partnership of responsibility with players. These are places that recognize that a quality golfing experience hinges not just on the *conditions* of play but also the *manner* of play. For the latter speaks to the spirit of the game and the promise of something pleasurable, not dreadful. Do players show respect for the course—such as repairing ball marks on greens and replacing divots in fairways—as much as they uphold the integrity of the game and display good sportsmanship with their playing partners? Whether riding in carts or walking, is the pace and conduct of play conducive to a truly enjoyable experience for all?

For what it ultimately comes down to is players choosing to model the behavior that they want to see in others. The enjoyment of the game, the good of the game, and, indeed, *the future* of the game are all at stake.

68

Milestones

Deep on the journey,
so many steps and shots past,
new milestones still loom

WHEN THE GAME was young to new players, the goals were simple, and so were the milestones that marked their achievement. First putt, first drive, first successful hit toward an intended target. First pair of golf shoes, first set of clubs, first swings on a real golf course.

With encouragement and interest, the milestones soon focused on the outcomes of the efforts. First eighteen hole round. First par. First birdie. First time breaking 100, then 90, then 80. First tournament victory. And although the odds are stacked 12,500 to 1 against the average golfer, first hole-in-one.

Yet golf hardly assures a linear progression to increased mastery. Although the National Golf Foundation reports that 55 percent of golfers in the United States will break 100, only 26 percent will break 90, and a much smaller number, 5 percent, 80. All this means that the average score for an amateur player hovers around 100 for eighteen holes.

Even so, that most extraordinary moment in the game—a hole-in-one—is available to every golfer, who, regardless of ability, launches a ball toward a green from a reachable tee box. Tiger Woods achieved his first at age 6; Michelle Wie at age 12. And Elsie McLean of Chico, California, got her first and only ace on the 100-yard-long fourth hole at Bidwell Park Golf Course on April 5, 2007. She was 102 and had been playing the game for nearly 80 years. Reflecting on the feat, Elsie clearly felt her time had come. "Well," she said, "everybody wants a hole-in-one. Why can't I have one?" Why not, indeed.

If age is not a limiting factor on a hole-in-one, it is a major element of another golfing milestone that many regard as an even more difficult feat—shooting one's age. The odds to do this, that is, to accomplish in an eighteen-hole round on a course of at least six thousand yards a score equaling or bettering a golfer's age, entirely depends on age, skill, and good health.

First, it is a feat for the not so young. Obviously, the older a golfer becomes, the more strokes are available to shoot one's age. This suggests that the achievement is easier to realize in your seventies or beyond than in your sixties.

But second, no matter what a player's age, the feat requires a high level of skill in the game. Only one in seven thousand golfers will ever shoot par for a full round in their lifetimes, but some do in remarkable ways. Bob Hamilton, the winner of the 1944 PGA Championship, shot 59 at age 59 in 1975. Bob Harris, a four-handicapper even in his mid-80s, accomplished the feat over a thousand times because his stroke average per round was 76. Even Harris was no match for Frank Bailey of Abilene, Texas, who, from age 71 until 98, recorded 2,623 rounds at or better than his age.

Third, and what all these players acknowledge, the feat requires both good physical health and a strong mental approach to the game. These factors enable continued golfing success even as one becomes older and the length of a player's shots gets shorter. Cardiovascular conditioning, strength training and flexibility, and building a game around accuracy and a solid short game are keys to enjoying the game into the years when shooting one's age can be more of a possibility.

Granted, with few exceptions, the window for this accomplishment is narrow. Not everyone has an ageless swing like Sam Snead, who accomplished the feat on the PGA tour with rounds of 67 and 66 in the Quad Cities Open in 1979 when he was 67. Nor the longevity of Arthur Thompson of Victoria, British Columbia, who became the oldest player to shoot his age when he was 103 years old.

But it is a milestone that still awaits many players after a lifetime of playing the game, and the odds do improve with age to reach it—at least theoretically.

69

Vitruvian Man

Leonardo's man,
blending mathematics and art—
mapping the golf swing.

L EONARDO DA VINCI'S magnificent and mesmerizing fifteenth-century drawing of a human male figure perfectly aligned within both a circle and a square is at the core of the artist's efforts to relate man to nature. The inspiration for his work was the examination of human proportionality by the first century BC Roman architect Marcus

Vitruvius Pollio, who believed that the basis for architectural design can be found in nature and nowhere more clearly than in the construct of the human body.

For both Vitruvius and Leonardo, the human form was more than a study of anatomy. It was, in fact, a celebration of what that form represented as an ideal analogy for understanding the workings and the symmetry of the universe. Its correlation to the immutable principles of geometry provided the basis for their argument and inspiration for their work. Thus, the *Vitruvian Man* is an image of greatness in two key ways. It reflects both the scientific and philosophical vision of the authors who developed it and illuminates the grand design of the Creator.

Golf was not in Leonardo's universe, of course, but its elements were. For here is an activity that hinges on understanding the workings of the human body and the principles of motion and movement relative to propelling an object across a natural landscape. It is about harmony between man and nature—and the quest to achieve it.

Beginning with Henry Brougham Farnie's *The Golfer's Manual* (1857), that quest has produced an extensive library of works committed to examining the game and providing guidance on how to play it. For the first century of such books, they could generally be characterized as playing tips from successful players, such as Harry Vardon, *How to Play Golf* (1907); Byron Nelson, *Winning Golf* (1946); and Bobby Jones, *Down the Fairway* (1927). This and other writings of Jones were subsequently adapted into a highly entertaining film series (*How I Play Golf*) that played in movie theaters before the main feature in the early 1930s. Said Jones about those films, they were "designed as instructive . . . (but not) so complicated that a non-golfer can't understand them."

Not surprisingly, the man who took golf instruction to another level was Ben Hogan with the publication of *Five Lessons: The Modern Fundamentals of Golf* in 1957. With assistance on the text from Herbert

Warren Wind and enhanced with the extraordinary drawings of Anthony Ravielli, Hogan translated the art and science of the *Vitruvian Man* to golf. The "visual instructions" that resulted from this collaboration powerfully conveyed the depth and precision of Hogan's understanding of the game and the painstaking requirements of its mastery. The book does not promise a quick fix or a short cut to lower scores, but it does provide a pathway to that goal.

And more. The book communicated the physical beauty and athleticism of the game. Indeed, there are certain images, such as a face-on view of a drawing of Hogan demonstrating stance and posture, complete with parallel lines that frame his shoulders and effect perfect balance (p. 41), that are as elegant and enthralling as Leonardo's beautifully proportioned and rendered subject.

To be sure, *Five Lessons* is the Hogan way. Just as Jack Nicklaus's *Golf My Way* (1974) is his and Tiger Woods' *How I Play Golf* (2008) is his. This is an important point about their books. For it is well to heed Bobby Jones' caution to recognize the distinction between the individual *mannerisms* of players and the golfing *fundamentals* they practiced. Often, a focus on the former can distract from the level of agreement on the latter. Rather, wrote Jones, "when we set side by side the playing methods of the best golfers, we always find that the basic movements and their orderly sequence are the same within a very narrow range."

But if neither Leonardo's circles and squares nor Hogan's planes and ellipses offer the secrets to a great swing, there are plenty of people and products claiming that they possess it. One of these is JC Anderson, a journeyman tour player from 1988 to 2013 who has spent most of his golfing career as a club professional. In a hilarious 2010 video, JC reveals the "ten secrets" or key swing thoughts that successful golf pros employ. Among several "vital" elements, these include the use and coordination of centripetal, lineal, and physical muscular force to snap load one's power package, amplify lag and drag pressure, avoid the breakdown of the number 2 power accumulator, and utilize the geometry of the circle. All this underscores that the golf swing can be divided into twenty-four components—each with twelve to fifteen variations. Clear?

Of course, all just clever satire . . . right?

70

Autumn

Indian summer—
a gift in the fading light
of the season's end.

A GOLFING SEASON CAN end abruptly. Sometimes it seems
that the seasonal passage to the fall hardly affords time to remember
the high skies and sunshine and long days that graced the rounds of
summer. Suddenly, the days are all twilight and a passing summer
shower or a short-lived thunderstorm has been replaced with rains that
arrive with blustery gusts and chilling temperatures and descend in
sheets. And last for days. In this autumn wind, even the wicker baskets
at Merion shudder and tremble.

The course has changed too. The remains of the last night's rain linger
longer in the autumn dew of cooler temperatures and dampened
grounds. Fallen leaves gather in bunkers and other eaves of the course
and intrude upon greens and fairways. The branches they abandoned
appear as skeletal arms and fingers against the sky. Yet upon them,
clearer than ever, a Cooper's hawk perches and scans for prey, which
has become more vulnerable in the withering rough and border areas
of the course in their early stages of dormancy.

It is a season ruthless in transition and rich in observation. All the more
so because the decrease of players as the year departs often leaves one

alone to pursue a round and to discover the pleasures of a different pace and scene.

And then just when everything seems so cold and stark, when the weeks of leaves move on and all color and comfort seem to be packed away for the winter, a warm, dry weekend defies the calendar. There is a mad rush to the course.

Amid heartening glances that these conditions augur well for an off-season that will allow more than an isolated round, players excitedly fill tee times and cautiously venture hopes; but of course, all is illusion. The reality of a false signal may be even more crushing than the barren branches above and the layers of wet leaves below.

Such days, though, do remind golfers how much they need their game, how much they rely upon it. It is an awareness that will buffer the boredom and ease the emptiness until everything begins again—as it must—in the spring.

71

Simplify

Before the first swing,
its images and lessons,
seek to simplify

" GOLF," SAID THE great amateur champion, Bobby Jones, "is the closest game to the game of life—you get bad breaks from good shots; you get good breaks from bad shots; but you have to play the ball where it lies."

Golfers and golf analysts have long examined and tested Jones' proposition as they have sought to understand the appeal and meaning of the game. They have particularly grappled with the intrinsic frustration of a game that offers neither perfection of play nor mastery of outcome. Again, Jones: "No one will ever have golf under his thumb. No round ever will be so good that it could not have been better."

Yet there are clues to finding one's place—and peace—in this game by asking a more fundamental question than which swing to choose or driver to buy or ball to play or shoes to wear. The biggest clue may be in what the game's most accomplished players say they do *before* they hit the ball rather than what happens when they strike it.

From Harry Vardon to Nick Faldo, Bobby Jones to Jack Nicklaus, there is remarkable consensus that success in the game depends on *a quiet mind.* That is, the ability to eliminate distractions and negative thoughts from the immediate task at hand. It is to *visualize* how the shot should perform, not let fear of its consequences dominate the process. It is to have, as Vardon said, "a *tranquil* frame of mind."

If the game of golf is like the game of life, then how a life is lived can influence how a game is played. Although Henry David Thoreau was clearly not contemplating his golf game when he took to a lake in the woods of Concord, Massachusetts, in 1845, he was seeking a pathway to a life less filled with complexity and distraction or, as he wrote, less "frittered away by detail." He summarized what he discovered during his two-year retreat with a simple mantra: "Simplify, simplify, simplify."[42]

For Thoreau, the key to happiness was rescuing a life from exhaustion and confusion from taking on too much and failing to grasp what truly matters in an otherwise busied and hurried existence. His two-year experience living in a cabin that he had constructed on the shore of Waldon Pond revealed not only the wonder of nature but also the freedom of simplicity. Not just for himself but for all who read his account of this adventure, he provided a compelling case for a life more in touch with simpler pleasures and inner strengths and a mind both more tranquil and disciplined.

Simplify. For golfers, Thoreau's admonition means not just matters of attitude and approach but also the physical requirements of the game, and there is remarkable consensus on the latter as well. Grip, stance, posture. It all begins with these fundamentals. As varied as golf swings may be, as divergent the idiosyncrasies and mannerisms that players bring to their games, there is basic agreement that swinging a golf club requires a sound understanding of its foundation elements: grip, stance, posture. Listen carefully to Thoreau's voice on the range: "As you simplify your life, the laws of the universe will be simpler." These include the laws of motion and movement that effect the golf swing and determine its consequences.

Simplify. For *haiku* poets, the words from the sage of Waldon Pond have compelled these writers to find power in simplicity. Of course, this has always been a goal of *haiku*, but contemporary *haiku* poets have experimented with ways to incorporate the elements and form of a three-line *haiku* into one line and fewer words and syllables. The late John Wills, for example, was a brilliant American *haiku* poet with a genius for simplicity of form, language, and imagery.[43] Like Thoreau, he found his inspiration through nature, which, in his case, involved living on a farm in the mountains of Tennessee.

Simplify. Guidance for life and poetry—and golf.

Tracks

Fresh tracks in deep tracks,
just enough to remind us
we've been here before

THE MORNING DEW holds the tracks of the first players of
the day. Well-worn pathways through dunes, upon hillsides,
and around waste areas mark where legions of golfers have pursued
their shots. Footprints in the woods, by the shallow edges of ponds, in
the trodden troughs along boundary fences, and among the debris of
beaches at low tide document where desperate searches for wayward
shots occurred. Some shoe marks in an unhappy location may even

look familiar to a golfer coming upon them. Perhaps they are his from a previous round or just a reason for a sigh of relief that there, but for the grace of God, could have been his own misfortune.

There are much deeper traces of the games that have been played on courses too, some visible, some not. Among the former are the plaques planted in the 18th fairways of both Merion and Baltusrol where Ben Hogan and Jack Nicklaus, respectively, hit 1-irons to the greens on the seventy-second holes of U.S. Opens they won. Hogan's shot from 213 yards ended up forty feet from the cup from where he two-putted to secure a spot in a play-off for the 1950 championship, which he won the next day over Lloyd Mangrum and George Fazio. The shot that Nicklaus made—the best long-iron, he said, he ever hit—flew 238 yards to the green for a closing birdie from twenty-two feet, a new record Open score of 275, and a four-shot margin of victory over runner-up Arnold Palmer in 1967.

These and similar others revive the deep tracks in our memories of the game.[44] For whether we have actually witnessed them or not, we are aware of their occurrence. They mean something to us. Not just a spectacular shot, a dramatic moment—but something deeper. They evoke pride in the champions of our sport, whose character, strength and vulnerability, passion and courage are laid bare in this game.

And something more. The rich narratives of the game that we store and recall effect communion with these heroes because we play the same game as they. No, not in the same manner or on the same skill level, but by the same rules, with the same history and traditions, often on the same courses, and with the same recognition that this is a game that will never be conquered but rarely abandoned.

For within this game is a strong infinity loop. Like a round of golf, the experience takes us to the far reaches of its design but returns us to its center. Within that journey there is common cause with our golfing companions, connection to the history and culture of the game, and both meaning and purpose in why we choose to play this game. And why we persist in doing so. Tournaments may finish and rounds may end, but the game never leaves us. Every round we play reminds us that we've been this way before—and readies us to go there again.

LIST OF ILLUSTRATIONS

GOLF PLAYERS AND PERSONALITIES NOTED

Tommy Aaron

Tip Anderson

Ian Baker-Finch

Rich Beem

John Burke

Harry S. Colt

Mike Cowan

Bing Crosby

Andrew Dickson

David Duval

Clint Eastwood

Ernie Els

George Fazio

William Flynn

Wayne Grady

Bob Hamilton

Padraig Harrington

Marion Hollins

Tony Jacklin

Bobby Jones

Tom Lehman

Eddie Lowery

Lloyd Mangrum

Charles Allison

Angelo Argea

Seve Ballesteros

Max Behr

Joe Carr

Jason Connery

Paula Creamer

Ben Curtis

Tom Doak

Pete Dye

Bruce Edwards

Nick Faldo

Tom Fazio

Jim Furyk

David Graham

Todd Hamilton

Bob Harris

"Shivas Irons"

Peter Jacobson

Tom Kite

Bobby Locke

Charles Blair
Macdonald

Andy Martinez

JC Anderson

Frank Bailey

Charles Banks

James Braid

Stewart Cink

Fred Couples

Ben Crenshaw

Bernard Darwin

Duke of York (James
II, England)

Alfred Dyer

Chandler Egan

Henry Brougham
Farnie

Jack Fleck

Molly Gourday

Walter Hagen

Butch Harmon

Ben Hogan

Hale Irwin

King James IV,
Scotland

Joe Lacava

Sheriff Logan

Alister Mackenzie

Mary, Queen
of Scots

Charles Maud John McDermott Jim McKay
Elsie McLean Terry McNamara Shaun Micheel
Phil Mickelson Johnny Miller Herman Mitchell
Orville Moody Old Tom Morris Young Tom Morris
Jay Morrish Michael Murphy Bill Murray
Tommy Nakajima Byron Nelson Jack Nicklaus
"Danny Noonan" Francis Ouimet Arnold Palmer
John Patersone Dave Peltz Harvey Penick
Maxwell Perry Gary Player Ted Ray
Seth Raynor Ricci Roberts Donald Ross
Bob Rotella Pat Ruddy Gene Sarazen
Charles Schulz Tom Simpson "Elihu Smails"
Sam Snead "Snoopy" Annika Sorenstam
"Carl Sprackler" Henrik Stenson Edward Stimpson
Prince Charles Fanny Sunesson John Sutherland
Edward Stuart
John Henry Taylor George C. Thomas Arthur Thompson
Peter Thompson Albert W. Tillinghast Lee Trevino
Harry Vardon Tom Watson "Ty Webb"
Tom Weiskopf Joyce Wethered Michelle Wie
Steve Williams Hugh Wilson Herbert Warren Wind

Tiger Woods

FEATURED COURSES

Augusta National, United States
Ballybunion (Old), Ireland
Bandon Dunes, United States
Bethpage (Black), United States
Brora, Scotland
Cabot Cliffs, Nova Scotia, Canada
Cabot Links, Nova Scotia, Canada
Chicago Golf Club, United States
Coeur d'Alene, United States
Cruden Bay, Scotland
Druid's Glen, Ireland
Estancia Club, United States
European Club, Ireland
Galen Hall, United States
Killarney Golf and Fishing Club, Ireland
Lahinch (Old), Ireland
La Quinta (Quarry Course), United States
Machrihanish (Old), Scotland
Merion (East), United States
North Berwick (West), Scotland
Old Course, St. Andrews, Scotland
Olympic Club, United States
Pebble Beach, United States
Pine Valley, United States
Prestwick, Scotland
Royal Burgess Golfing Society, Scotland
Royal County Down, Northern Ireland
Royal Dornoch, Scotland
Royal Liverpool, England
Shadow Creek, United States
Tournament Players Club (Sawgrass), United States

NOTED COURSES

Adare Golf Club, Ireland
Arcadia Bluffs, United States
Ardglass, Northern Ireland
Ballybunion (Cashen), Ireland
Baltusrol (Lower), United States
Banff Springs, Alberta, Canada
Barndougle Dunes, Tasmania, New Zealand
Barndougle Lost Farm, Tasmania, New Zealand
Bay Hill, United States
Bayside Links, United States
Beaver Tail Golf Club, United States
Bidwell Park Golf Course, United States
Blairgowie (Rosemount Course), Scotland
"Burningbush Golf Links," Scotland
"Bushwood Country Club," United States
Carnoustie, Scotland
Castle Stuart, Scotland
Chambers Bay, United States
Concord Resort (Monster), United States
Cork Golf Club, Ireland
Country Club (Brookline), United States
Crail Golfing Society (Balcomie Links), Scotland
Crystal Downs, United States
Cypress Point, United States
Deepdale Golf Club, United States
Del Monte, United States
Desert Highlands, United States
Doonbeg, Ireland
Doral (Blue), United States
Erin Hills, United States

Fort Washington, United States
Gleneagles (King's and Queen's Courses), Scotland
Grayhawk Golf Club, United States
Gullen (No. 1), Scotland
Hachioji Country Club, Japan
Haggin Oaks, United States
Hanglip Mountain, South Africa
Hangman Golf Club, United States
Harbour Town, United States
Hell's Point Golf Club, United States
Hirono Golf Club, Japan
Hourin Country Club, Japan
Island Club, Ireland
Jockey Club, Argentina
Kaganei Golf Club, Japan
Kapalua (Plantation Course), United States
Kasumigaseki Country Club, Japan
Kawana Golf Course, Japan
Kiawah Island (Ocean Course), United States
Kingsbarns, Scotland
Ko'olau, United States
La Quinta (Mountain Course), United States
Lido Golf Club, United States
Machrihanish Links, Scotland
Meadow Club, United States
Mill Road Farm Country Club, United States
Mission Bay, United States
Nairn, Scotland
Naruo Golf Club, Japan
National Golf Links of America, United States
Nightmare Golf Course, United States
Oakmont, United States
Old Head, Ireland
Old Macdonald, United States
Ome Golf Club, Japan

Pacific Dunes, United States

Pasatiempo, United States

Pinehurst (No. 2), United States

Portmarnoch, Ireland

Prairie Dunes, United States

Pumpkin Ridge (Ghost Creek Course), United States

Purgatory Golf Club, United States

Pyongyang Golf Club, North Korea

Riviera, United States

Rosapenna, Ireland

Royal Adelaide, Australia

Royal Birkdale, England

Royal Lytham and St. Annes, England

Royal Musselburgh, Scotland

Royal North Devon (Westward Ho!), England

Royal Portrush, Northern Ireland

Royal St. Georges, England

Royal Troon (Portland Course), Scotland

Shinnecock, United States

Spanish Bay, United States

Spyglass, United States

Tama Country Club, Japan

Tralee Golf Club, Ireland

Troon North (Monument Course), United States

Turnberry (Ailsa), Scotland

Valley Club, United States

Waterville, Ireland

Westhampton Country Club, United States

Whirlwind Golf Club (Devil's Claw Course), United States

Whistling Straits, United States

White Witch, Jamaica

Winged Foot, United States

Yale University Golf Course, United States

Yomiuri Country Club, Japan

SELECTED SOURCES AND BIBLIOGRAPHY

HAIKU

Addiss, Stephen. *The Art of Haiku: Its History Through Poems and Paintings by Japanese Masters.* Boston and New York: Shambala, 2012.

_____. *A Haiku Garden: The Four Seasons in Poems and Prints.* New York: Weatherhill, 1996.

_____. *Haiku Landscapes: In Sun, Wind, Rain, and Snow.* New York: Weatherhill, 2002.

Aitken, Robert. *A Zen Wave: Basho's Haiku and Zen.* New York: Weatherhill, 2009.

Atwood, Ann. *Haiku-Vision in Poetry and Photography.* New York: Scribner, 1977.

Basho, Matsuo. *The Essential Basho.* Trans. Sam Hamill. Boston and London: Shambala, 1998.

_____. *The Narrow Road to the Deep North and Other Travel Sketches.* Trans. Nobuyuki Yuasa. New York: Penguin, 1966.

Beichman, Janine. *Masaoka Shiki.* Boston: Twayne Publishers, 1982.

Blythe, R. H. *A History of Haiku: Volume One, From the Beginnings Up to Issa.* Tokyo: Hokuseido, 1963.

Bowers, Faubion. Editor. *The Classic Tradition of Haiku: An Anthology.* Mineola, NY: Dover, 1996.

Brandi, John and Dennis Maloney. Editors. *The Unswept Path: Contemporary American Haiku.* New York: White Pine Press, 2005.

Carter, Steven. *Traditional Japanese Poetry: An Anthology.* Stanford, CA: Stanford University Press, 1991.

Collins, Billy. *She Was Just Seventeen: Haiku.* Lee Gurga, editor. Lincoln, IL: Modern *Haiku* Press, 2006.

de Christoforo, Violet. *May Sky – There's Always Tomorrow: A History and Anthology of Haiku.* Los Angeles: Sun and Moon Press, 1996.

Donegan, Patricia. *Haiku Mind: 108 Poems to Cultivate Awareness and Open Your Heart.* Boston and London: Shambala, 2010.

French, Calvin L. *The Poet-Painters: Buson and His Followers.* Ann Arbor, MI: University of Michigan Museum of Art, 1974.

Gilbert, Richard. *Poems of Consciousness: Contemporary Japanese and English Language Haiku in Cross-Cultural Perspective.* Winchester, VA: Red Moon Press, 2008.

Giroux, Joan. *The Haiku Form.* Rutland, VT: Tuttle, 1974.

Gurga, Lee. *Haiku: A Poet's Guide.* Lincoln, IL: Modern Haku Press, 2007.

Hall, John Whitney. Translator. *The Sound of Water: Haiku by Basho, Buson, Issa and Other Poets.* Boston and London: Shambala, 1995.

Hamill, Sam. Editor and translator. *The Pocket Haiku.* Boston and London: Shambala, 2014.

Hass, Robert. Editor and translator. *The Essential Haiku: Versions of Basho, Buson, & Issa.* Hopewell, NJ: Ecco Press, 1994.

Heaney, Seamus. *Our Shared Japan.* Dublin: Dedalus Press, 2007.

Henderson, Harold G. *An Introduction to Haiku: An Anthology of Poems and Poets from Basho to Shiki.* New York: Doubleday, 1958.

Higginson, William J. and Penny Harter. *The Haiku Handbook: How to Write, Share and Teach Haiku.* New York: McGraw-Hill, 1985.

_____. Editor. *The Haiku Seasons: Poetry of the Natural World.* Tokyo: Kodansha International, 1996.

_____. Editor. *Haiku World: An International Poetry Almanac.* Tokyo: Kodansha International, 1996.

Issa, Kobayashi. *The Autumn Wind: A Selection from the Poems of Issa.* Trans. Lewis Mackenzie. Tokyo and New York: Kodansha International, 1984.

_____. *A Year in My Life.* Trans. Nobuyuki Yausa. Berkeley: University of California Press, 1972.

Kacian, Jim and Philip Rowland, Allan Burns. Editors. *Haiku in English: The First Hundred Years.* New York: W. W. Norton, 2013.

Kata, Koko. Editor and translator. *A Hidden Pond: Anthology of Modern Haiku*. Tokyo: Kadokawa Shoten, 1997.

Keene, Donald. *Landscapes and Portraits: Appreciations of Japanese Culture*. Tokyo: Kodansha International, 1971.

_____. *World Without Walls: Japanese Lirerature of the Pre-Modern Era, 1600-1868*. New York: Grove Press, 1976.

Kerouac, Jack. *The Book of Haikus*. Regina Weinreich, editor. New York: Penguin, 2003.

Lowenstein, Tom. Editor. *Classic Haiku: The Greatest Japanese Poetry from Basho, Busan, Issa, Shiki and Their Followers*. New York; Shelter Harbor Press, 2016.

Manheim, Ron. *Haiku & Haiga: Moments in Word and Image*. Amsterdam: Hotei, 2006.

Mayhew, Lenore. *Monkey's Raincoat: Linked Poetry of the Basho School with Haiku Selections*. Rutland, VT: Tuttle, 1985.

Miner, Earl. *Japanese Linked Poetry*. Princeton, NJ: Princeton University Press, 1980.

_____. *The Monkey's Straw Raincoat*. Princeton, NJ: Princeton University Press, 1981.

_____ and Hiroko Odagiri, Robert E. Morrell. Editors. *The Princeton Companion to Classical Japanese Literature*. Princeton, NJ: Princeton University Press, 1985.

Miyamori, Asataro. *An Anthology of Haiku, Ancient and Modern*. Tokyo: Chugai Printing Co., 1932).

Moore, James. *The Haiku Companion*. Bloomington, IN: iUniverse, 2012.

Pratt, Judith, Michiko Wankentyne, Barry Till. *Haiku: Japanese Art and Poetry*. Petaluma, CA: Pomegranate Communications, 2010.

Reichold, Jane. Translator. *Basho: The Complete Haiku*. Tokyo: Kodansha, 2008.

_____. *Writing and Enjoying Haiku: A Hands-on Guide*. New York: Kodansha, 2002.

Rexroth, Kenneth. Translator. *One Hundred Poems from the Japanese*. New York: New Directions, 1956.

Rimer. J. Thomas. *A Reader's Guide to Japanese Literature.* Tokyo: Kodansha International, 1988.

Ross, Bruce. Editor. *Haiku Moment: An Anthology of Contemporary North American Haiku.* Rutland, VT: Charles E. Tuttle, 1993.

Sato, Hiroaki. *One Hundred Frogs: From Renga to Haiku to English.* New York: Weatherhill, 1983.

_____ and Burton Watson. Editors. *From the Country of Eight Islands: An Anthology of Japanese Poetry.* Seattle, WA: University of Washington Press, 1981.

Sawa, Yuki and Edith M. Shiffert. *Haiku Master Buson.* South SF: Heian International, 1978.

Shiki, Masaoka. *Selected Poems.* Trans. Nobuyuki Yausa. New York: Columbia University Press, 1997.

Shirane, Haruo. *Early Modern Japanese Literature: An Anthology, 1600-1900.* New York: Columbia University Press, 2008.

_____. *Traces of Dreams: Landscape, Cultural Memory, and the Poetry of Basho.* Stanford, CA: Stanford University Press, 1998.

Stryk, Lucien. *On Love and Barley: Haiku by Basho.* London: Penguin Books, 1985.

Suzuki, Daisetz. *Zen and Japanese Culture.* New York: Princeton University Press, 1959.

Ueda, Makoto. *Basho and His Interpreters: Selected Hokku with Commentary.* Stanford, CA: Stanford University Press, 1991.

_____. *Dew on the Grass: The Life and Poetry of Kobayashi Issa.* Leiden: Brill, 2004.

_____. Editor and translator. *Modern Japanese Haiku: An Anthology.* Toronto: University of Toronto Press, 1976.

_____. *The Path of Flowering Thorn: The Life and Poetry of Yosa Buson.* Stanford, CA: Stanford University Press, 1998.

van den Heuvel, Cor. Editor. *The Haiku Anthology: Haiku and Senryu in English.* New York: W.W. Norton, 1999.

_____ and Nanae Tamura, Editors. *Baseball Haiku: The Best Haiku Ever Written About the Game.* New York: W. W. Norton, 2007.

_____and Tom Lynch, Michael Dylan Welch. Editors. *Wedge of Light*. Foster City, CA: Press Here, 1999.

Washington, Peter. *Haiku*. New York: Knopf, 2003.

Wills, John. *Up a Distant Ridge*. Manchester, NH: First *Haiku* Press, 1980.

Wright, Richard. *Haiku: The Last Poems of an American Icon*. New York: Arcade, 1998.

_____. *Haiku: This Other World*. New York: Arcade, 1998.

Yasuda, Kenneth. *The Japanese Haiku: Its Essential Nature, History, and Possibilities in English*. Rutland, VT: Tuttle, 1957.

Zolbrod, Leon M. *Haiku Painting*. Tokyo: Kodansha, 1982.

GOLF

Alison, Charles and Harry S. Colt. *Some Essays on Golf Course Architecture*. London: Country Life and George Newnes, 1920.

Allen, Peter. *Famous Fairways*. London: Stanley Paul, 1968.

_____. *Play the Best Courses: Great Golf in the British Isles*. London: Stanley Paul, 1973, revised 1987.

Bamberger, Michael. *Men in Green*. New York: Simon & Schuster, 2015.

Barrett, David. *Golf Courses of the U. S. Open*. New York: Abrams, 2007.

_____. *Making the Masters: Bobby Jones and the Birth of America's Greatest Golf Tournament*. New York: Skyhorse, 2012.

_____. *Miracle at Merion*. New York: Skyhorse, 2012.

Bauer, Alex. *Hazards: Those Essential Elements in a Golf Course Without Which the Game Would be Tame and Uninteresting*. Chicago: Tony Rubovits, 1913.

Bohan, Rachel and Heather Medlock, Editors. *The Art of Golf*. Atlanta, GA: High Museum of Art, 2012.

Browning, Robert. *A History of Golf: The Royal and Ancient Game*. London: J. M. Dent, 1955.

Callahan, Tom (with Tiger Woods). *In Search of Tiger: A Journey Through Golf*. New York: Crown, 2003.

Cook, Kevin. *Tommy's Honor: The Story of Old Tom Morris and Young Tom Morris, Golf's Founding Father and Son.* New York: Gotham Books, 2007.

Cornish, Geoffrey S. and Ronald Whitten. *The Architects of Golf.* New York: Harper-Collins, 1993.

_____. *The Golf Course.* New York: Rutledge, 1981.

Daley, Paul. Compiler and editor. *Golf Architecture: A Worldwide Perspective.* 2 vols. Gretna: Pelican, 2003.

Diaz, Jaime and Linda Harbaugh, Illustrator. *Hallowed Ground: Golf's Greatest Places.* Shelton, CT: Greenwich Workshop Press, 1999.

Daley, Paul. *Golf Architecture: A Worldwide Perspective.* Melbourne: Full Swing Golf Publishing, 2002.

Darwin, Bernard. *The Golf Courses of the British Isles.* London: Duckworth, 1910.

_____. *A History of Golf in Britain.* London: Cassell, 1952.

_____. *James Braid.* London: Hodder and Stoughton, 1952.

_____ and Jeff Silverman. *Bernard Darwin on Golf.* Guilford, CT: Lyons, 2003.

Davis, William H. *et al. 100 Greatest Golf Courses – And then Some.* Norwalk, CT: Golf Digest/Tennis Inc., 1982.

Dickinson, Patric. *A Round of Golf Courses.* London: Evans Brothers Ltd., 1950.

Doak, Tom. *The Anatomy of a Golf Course: The Art of Golf Architecture.* New York: Lyons and Burford, 1992.

_____. *The Confidential Guide to Golf Courses.* Chelsea, MI: Sleeping Bear Press, 1996.

_____, James S. Scott and Raymond M. Haddock. *The Life and Work of Dr. Alister MacKenzie.* Chelsea, MI: Sleeping Bear Press, 2001.

Dodson, James. *Ben Hogan: An American Life.* New York: Random House, 2004.

Edmund, Nick. *Classic Golf Courses of Great Britain and Ireland.* Boston: Little, Brown, 1997.

Elliot, Alan and John Allan May. *The Illustrated History of Golf.* London: Hamlyn, 1990.

Fay, Michael J. *Golf, As It Was Meant To Be Played: A Celebration of Donald Ross's Vision of the Game.* New York: Universe Publishing, 2000.

Fazio, Tom (with Cal Brown). *Golf Course Designs.* New York: Abrams, 2000.

Feinstein, John. *A Good Walk Spoiled: Days and Nights on the PGA Tour.* Boston: Little, Brown, 1995.

_____. *The Majors.* Boston: Little, Brown, 1999.

Finegan, James W. *Blasted Heaths and Blessed Greens: A Golfer's Pilgrimage to the Courses of Scotland.* New York: Simon & Schuster, 1996.

_____. *A Centennial Tribute to Golf in Philadelphia: The Champions and the Championships, the Clubs and the Courses.* Philadelphia: Golf Association of Philadelphia, 1996.

_____. *Emerald Fairways and Foam-Flecked Seas: A Golfer's Pilgrimage to the Courses of Ireland.* New York: Simon & Schuster, 1996.

Finn, George A. *Lazy Days at Lahinch.* Chelsea, MI: Sleeping Bear Press, 2002.

_____. *Through the Green, Lightly.* Lahinch, Ireland: Golfinn Publications, 1997.

Frost, Mark. *The Grand Slam: Bobby Jones, America, and the Story of Golf.* New York: Hyperion, 2004.

_____. *The Greatest Game Ever Played: Harry Vardon, Francis Ouimet, and the Birth of Modern Golf.* New York: Hyperion, 2002.

Goodwin, Stephen. *Dream Golf: The Making of Bandon Dunes.* Chapel Hill, NC: Algonquin, 2006.

Hamilton, David. *The Good Golf Guide to Scotland.* Edinburgh: Canongate Publishing, 1982.

Hauser, Thomas. *Arnold Palmer: A Personal Journey.* San Francisco: Collins Publishers, 1994.

Hawtree, Frederick W. *Colt & Co.* Oxford: Cambuc Archive, 1991.

Henderson, Ian and David I. Stirk. *Golf in the Making.* London: Sean Arnold, 1982.

Hogan, Ben (with Herbert Warren Wind). *Five Lessons: The Modern Fundamentals of Golf.* New York: Simon & Schuster, 1957.

Hunter, Robert. *The Links.* New York: Scribner's, 1926.

Hurdzan, Michael. *Golf Course Architecture.* Chelsea, MI: Sleeping Bear Press, 1996.

Hutchinson, Horace G. *The Badminton Library: Golf.* London: Longmans, Green, 1892.

_____. *British Golf Links.* London: J.S. Virtue, 1897.

Jarrett, Tom. *St. Andrews Golf Links: The First 600 Years.* Edinburgh: Mainstream Publishing, 1995.

Jenkins, Dan. *Sports Illustrated's the Best 18 Golf Holes in America.* New York: Delacorte, 1966.

Jones, Bobby. *Golf is My Game.* Garden City, NY: Doubleday, 1960.

Jones, Robert Trent, Jr. *Golf by Design.* New York: Little, Brown, 1993.

Joy, David. *The Scrapbook of Old Tom Morris.* Chelsea, MI: Sleeping Bear Press, 2001.

Keeler, O. B. *The Bobby Jones Story: The Authorized Biography.* Chicago: Triumph, 2003.

Kirk, John and Timothy Jacobs. Editors. *The Golf Courses of Robert Trent Jones, Jr.* New York: Gallery Books, 1988.

Kirsch, George B. *Golf in America.* Urbana: University of Illinois Press, 2009.

Klein, Bradley. *Discovering Donald Ross: The Architect and His Courses.* Chelsea, MI: Sleeping Bear Press, 2001.

_____. *Rough Meditations.* Chelsea, MI: Sleeping Bear Press, 1997.

Kroeger, Robert. *The Golf Courses of Old Tom Morris.* Cincinnati: Heritage Communications, 1995.

Labbance, Bob. *The Vardon Invasion: Harry's Triumphant 1900 American Tour.* Ann Arbor, MI: Sports Media Group, 2008.

Lewis, Catherine M. *Bobby Jones and the Quest for the Grand Slam.* Chicago: Triumph Books, 2005.

_____. *Considerable Passions: Golf, The Masters and the Legacy of Bobby Jones.* Chicago: Triumph Books, 2000.

Lewis, Peter. *Professional Golf, 1819-1885.* St. Andrews, Scotland: Royal and Ancient Golf Club of St. Andrews, 1998.

Lowe, Steven. *Sir Walter and Mr. Jones: Walter Hagen, Bobby Jones, and the Rise of American Golf.* Chelsea, MI: Sleeping Bear Press, 2000.

Macdonald, Charles Blair. *Scotland's Gift, Golf: Reminiscences, 1872-1927.* New York: Scribner's, 1928.

Machat, Udo and Cal Brown. *The Golf Courses of the Monterey Peninsula.* New York: Simon & Schuster, 1989.

MacKenzie, Alister. *Golf Architecture: Economy in Course Construction and Green-Keeping.* London: Simpkin, Marshall, Hamilton, Kent, 1920.

_____. *The Spirit of St. Andrews.* Chelsea, MI: Sleeping Bear Press, 1995.

Mackenzie, Richard. *A Wee Nip at the 19th Hole: A History of the St. Andrews Caddie.* Chelsea, MI: Sleeping Bear Press, 1997.

Mackie, Keith. *Golf at St. Andrews.* London: Arum Press, 1995.

Mair, Norman. *Muirfield: Home of the Honourable Company (1744-1994).* Edinburgh: Mainstream, 1994.

Matthew, Sid. *The Life and Times of Bobby Jones.* Chelsea, MI: Sleeping Bear Press, 1995.

Mayo, James M. *The American Country Club: Its Origins and Development.* New Brunswick, NJ: Rutgers University Press, 1998.

McCord, Robert. Editor. *The Quotable Golfer.* New York: Lyons Press, 2000.

McGuire, Brenda and John. *Golf at the Water's Edge: Scotland's Seaside Links.* New York: Abbeville Press, 1997.

Miracle, Louise and Rick. *Trolleys and Squibs: A Golfer's Guide to Ireland.* San Francisco: Pomegranate Communications, 2009.

Moss, Richard J. *The Kingdom of Golf in America.* Lincoln, NE: University of Nebraska Press, 2013.

Murphy, Michael. *Golf in the Kingdom.* New York: Viking, 1972.

Nelson, Byron. *How I Played the Game: An Autobiography.* New York: Dell, 1993.

Nicklaus, Jack (with Ken Bowden). *Golf My Way.* New York: Simon & Schuster, 1974.

_____ and Ken Bowden. *Jack Nicklaus: My Story*. New York: Simon & Schuster, 1997.

_____ and Chris Millard. *Golf by Design: Golf Course Strategy and Architecture*. New York: Harry N. Abrams, 2002.

Ouimet, Francis. *A Game of Golf: A Book of Reminiscences*. Boston: Houghton Mifflin, 1932.

Palmer, Arnold. *A Life Well Played: My Stories*. New York: St. Martin's Press, 2016.

_____ (with James Dodson). *A Golfer's Life*. New York: Ballantine Books, 1999.

Parkes, Marty. *Classic Shots: The Greatest Images from the United States Golf Association*. Washington, DC: National Geographic Society, 2007.

Penick, Harvey (with Bud Shrake). *Harvey Penick's Little Red Book*. New York: Simon & Schuster, 1992.

Peper, George. *St. Andrews Sojourn: Two Years at Home on the Old Course*. New York: Simon & Schuster, 2006.

_____. Editor. *Golf in America: The First One Hundred Years*. New York: Harry N. Abrams, 1994.

_____ et al. *The 500 World's Greatest Holes*. New York: Artisan, 2000.

Platts, Mitchell. *The Illustrated History of Golf*. New York: Gramercy, 2000.

Price, Charles. *The World of Golf*. New York: Random House, 1962.

Price, Robert. *Scotland's Golf Courses*. Edinburgh: Aberdeen University Press, 1989.

Redmond, John. *Great Golf Courses of Ireland*. Dublin: Gill & Macmillan, 1992.

Rowlinson, Mark. *Golfing on the World's Most Exceptional Courses*. New York: Abbeville Press, 2005.

Ross, Donald J. *Golf Has Never Failed Me*. Chelsea, MI: Sleeping Bear Press, 1997.

Rotella, Bob. *Golf is Not a Game of Perfect*. New York: Simon & Schuster, 1995.

Rubenstein, Lorne. *A Season in Dornoch: Golf and Life in the Scottish Highlands*. Edinburgh and London: McClelland & Stewart, 2001.

Ruddy, Pat. *Fifty Years in a Bunker: The Creation of a World Top-100 Golf Links at The European Club*. Brittas Bay, Ireland: Ruddy Golf Library, 2007.

_____. *The Perfect Golf Links: The Links of the European Club in Pictures with Musings on Golf Architecture*. Brittas Bay, Ireland: Ruddy Golf Library, 2012.

Schackleford, Geoff. *The Golden Age of Golf Design*. Chelsea, MI: Sleeping Bear Press, 1999.

_____. Editor. *Masters of the Links: Essays on the Art of Golf and Course Design*. Chelsea, MI: Sleeping Bear Press, 1997.

Schwartz, Gary H. *The Art of Golf, 1754-1940*. Tiburon, CA: Wood River Publishing, 1990.

Scott, Tim. *Ben Hogan: The Myths Everyone Knows, The Man No One Knew*. Chicago: Triumph Books, 2015.

Shields, Michael Patrick. *Secrets of the Great Golf Course Architects: The Creation of the World's Greatest Golf Courses in the Words and Images of History's Master Designers*. New York: Skyhorse, 2015.

Silverman, Jeff. *Merion: The Championship Story*. West Chester, PA: ANRO Communications, 2013.

Smith, Donald L. and John P. Holms. *The Gods of Golf*. New York: Simon & Schuster, 1996.

Sorenstam, Annika. *Golf Annika's Way: How I Elevated My Game to Be the Best: And How You Can, Too*. New York: Penguin, 2004.

Steel, Donald. *Classic Golf Links of England, Scotland, Wales and Ireland*. Gretna, LA: Pelican, 1993.

Stirk, David. *Carry Your Bag, Sir? A History of Golf's Caddies*. London: Witherby, 1992.

_____. *Golf: The Great Club Makers*. London: Witherby, 1992.

_____. *Golf: The History of an Obsession*. Oxford: Phaidon Press, 1987.

Taylor, Dawson. *St. Andrews: Cradle of Golf*. Cranbury, NJ: A. S. Barnes, 1976.

Thomas, George C., Jr. *Golf Architecture in America: Its Strategy and Construction*. Los Angeles: Times-Mirror Press, 1927.

Tillinghast, A. W. *The Course Beautiful*. Lynchburg, VA: TreeWolf Productions, 1995.

Tolhurst, Desmond and Gary A. Galyean. *Golf at Merion*. Ardmore, PA: Merion Golf Club, 2005.

Tufts, Richard S. *The Principles Behind the Rules of Golf*. United States Golf Association, 1960.

Vardon, Harry. *The Complete Golfer*. New York: McClure, Phillips, 1905.

Ward-Thomas, Pat. *The Royal and Ancient*. Edinburgh: Scottish Academic Press, 1980.

_____ et al. *The World Atlas of Golf*. London: Mitchell Beazley, 1976.

Wethered, H. N. and T. Simpson. *The Architectural Side of Golf*. London: Longmans, 1929.

Wexler, Daniel. *The Book of Golfers: A Biographical History of the Royal & Ancient Game*. Ann Arbor, MI: Sports Media Group, 2005.

_____. *Missing Links: America's Greatest Lost Golf Courses & Holes*. Chelsea, MI: Sleeping Bear Press, 2000.

Williams, Bill. *Vardon in America*. Bloomington, IN: Xlibris Publishing, 2016.

Wind, Herbert Warren. *Following Through*. New York: Ticknor and Fields, 1985.

_____. *The Story of American Golf: Its Champions and Its Championships*. New York: Knopf, 1975.

Zingg, Paul J. *An Emerald Odyssey: In Search of the Gods of Golf and Ireland*. Cork, Ireland: Collins Press, 2008.

_____. *A Good Round: A Journey Through the Landscapes and Memory of Golf*. Danbury, CT: Rutledge, 1999.

ENDNOTES

1   Although he came later, Masaoka Shiki (1867–1902) is also considered one of the Four Great Masters of haiku along with Basho, Buson, and Issa. He is acknowledged as the first "modern" *haiku* poet and was the first to describe his poetry as *haiku*. He devoted his life to promoting *haiku* and coveted his identity as a *haijin*, or "*haiku* person," that is, a dedicated *haiku* poet.

2   Faubion Bowers, Editor, *The Classic Tradition of Haiku: Anthology* (Mineola, NY: Dover Publications, 1996), 15.

3   The literature of "the inner game" includes such works as Tim Gallwey, *The Inner Game of Golf* (1981); Bob Rotella, *Golf Is Not a Game of Perfect* (1995); Fred Shoemaker, *Extraordinary Golf: The Art of the Possible* (1996); Joseph Parent, *Zen Golf: Mastering the Mental Game* (2002); Harvey Penick, *Harvey Penick's Little Red Book: Lessons and Teachings from a Lifetime in Golf* (1991); Patrick Cohn, *Going Low: How to Break Your Individual Golf Scoring Barrier by Thinking Like a Pro* (2001); Gio Valiante, *Fearless Golf: Conquering the Mental Game* (2005); and the fictional classic, Michael Murphy, *Golf in the Kingdom* (1972).

4   Hamill, *The Pocket Haiku* (Boston and London: Shambhala, 2014), xiii–xiv, xvii–xviii; and *The Sound of Water: Haiku by Basho, Buson, Issa and Other Poets* (Boston and London: Shambhala, 1995).

5   There is a form of Japanese *haiku*-based literature called *haibun*, which translates as "*haiku* prose." And again, Basho was its first master in his great travel journal, *Oku no Hosomichi* (Narrow Road to the North). This expression combines some prose with the *haiku*, wherein the poem serves as an epilogue to the prose element of the complete piece. Like *haiku*, *haibun* has a set of rules and characteristics that pivot on brevity and a balance between connecting the poem and the essay and, at the same time, maintaining a certain detachment. While this book more clearly embraces *haiku* than *haibun*, it acknowledges the effectiveness of *haibun* in conveying the impressions and experiences that are recorded in travel journals and diaries. For this book is a *journey* of sorts inviting the reader to consider the discoveries of the author in the quest for a deeper understanding of one's place in the game that connects us.

6   Kacian, quoted in Kacian, Philip Rowland, Allan Burns, Editors, *Haiku in English: The First Hundred Years* (New York: Norton, 2013), 333.

7   Billy Collins, *Haiku in English*, xxx.

8   Van Morrison, music and lyrics, "Into the Mystic," first recorded 1969.

9   Yeats, "A Prayer for my Daughter" (1919).

10 Sandburg, "Fog" (1916).

11 Smith, "Fog" (1975).

12 Michael Murphy, *Golf in the Kingdom* (New York: Viking, 1972), Chapter 4, "Singing the Praises of Golf."

13 "A baggepype wel coude he blowe and sowne, and ther-with-al he broghte us out of towne," quoted in Chaucer, *The Canterbury Tales* (circa 1380), "Prologue to 'The Millers Tale,'" line 565.

14 Updike, Foreword, Charles Lindsay, *Lost Balls: Great Holes, Tough Shots, and Bad Lies* (New York: Bulfinch Press, 2005).

15 An alternative to the USGA *Rules of Golf* that covers many lost ball scenarios is Henry Beard, *The Official Rules of Bad Golf* (New York: Sterling Publishing, 2006). Beard provides "a complete set of simple, commonsense, stroke-saving rules for the game that *most* of us play." They include eighteen "generally accepted Mulligans" and twelve "blanket waivers from penalty strokes," such as "Ball Playable in Water Hazard, but Just Not Worth It," "Ball Hit Slightly Out-of-Bounds," and "Ball Missing in Fairway, but Obviously Not Lost."

16 MacKenzie, *Golf Architecture: Economy of Course Construction and Green-Keeping* (London: Simpkin, Marshall, Hamilton, Kent, 1920), 39.

17 Quoted in Tom Doak, *The Anatomy of a Golf Course* (New York: Lyons & Burford, 1992), 135.

18 The inspiration for the film is Kevin Cook's history, *Tommy's Honor: The Story of Old Tom and Young Tom Morris: Golf's Founding Father and Son* (New York: Gotham Books, 2007). Cook also served as a screenwriter for the film along with his wife, Pamela Marin. The film received the 2016 Best Picture Award by the British Academy Scotland. Cook's book won the United States Golf Association Herbert Warren Wind Book Award in 2007 and was named one of the five best "Books of the Year" in 2007 by *Sports Illustrated*.

19 Logan, "Far and Sure" in Robert Clark, Editor, *Golf: A Royal and Ancient Game* (London: Macmillan, 1893), 218.

20 The Fourth Industrial Revolution (4IR) builds on the "digital revolution" that has been occurring since the mid-twentieth century. It is characterized by the fusion of technologies and disciplines that increasingly crosses the boundaries between the physical, digital, and biological. Its implications for golf flow from technological breakthroughs and innovation in such areas as 3-D printing, biotechnology, materials science, robotics, virtual reality, and immersive video gaming.

21 As did 64-year-old Mike Austin, when, competing in the 1974 Senior National Open Qualifier, he smashed his steel-shafted persimmon head driver 516 yards. It is the longest drive ever recorded in a regular golf competition. For specialized long drive events, the contestants often exceed 400 yards, although the average winning distance is about 360 yards.

22 Joseph O'Connor, *The Secret World of the Irish Male* (Dublin: New Island Books, 1994), 144.

23 Joe Carr, "Welcome to Irish Golf" in Louise and Rick Miracle, *Trolleys and Squibs: A Golfer's Guide to Irish Links* (San Francisco: Pomegranate, 2000), 9.

24 Richard Finney and Scott Whitley, *Links of Heaven: A Complete Guide to Golf Journeys in Ireland* (Ogdensburg, NY: Baltray Books, 1996), 200.

25 Excellent analysis of this data is provided by L. J. Riccio, "Statistical Analysis of the Average Golfer" in Alastair J. Cochran, Editor, *Science and Golf: Proceedings of the First World Scientific Conference on Golf* (London: E & FN Spon, 1990), 153–158; and Mark Brodie, "Assessing Golfer Performance on the PGA Tour," *Interfaces*, vol. 42, no. 12 (March–April, 2012), 146–165.

26 Simpson's other highly regarded courses include Carlow Golf Club and County Louth Golf Club (Ireland), Morfantaine Golf Club and Fontainebleau Golf Club (France), and the New Zealand Golf Club and Marlborough Golf Club (England). His partnership with William Herbert Fowler, who was regarded by the golf historian, Bernard Darwin, as "perhaps the most daring and original of all golfing architects," no doubt had a great influence on his design career.

27 Wind, "North to the Links of Dornoch," *The New Yorker*, June 6, 1964.

28 The 2016–2017 golf course rankings by *Golf Digest* list Royal Dornoch as number 1 in Scotland, number 2 in the United Kingdom (behind only Royal County Down in Northern Ireland), and number 5 in the world (behind Royal County Down, Augusta National, Pine Valley, and Cypress Point).

29 In 2000, Tiger Woods matched Hogan's feat of three Majors (and three consecutively) in a single year with victories in the U.S. Open, the Open Championship, and PGA Championship. He opened the 2001 Major season with a win at the Masters, thus holding all four Major titles at the same time, although not garnered in a single year. His accomplishment has been dubbed the "Tiger Slam."

30 The total number of Major championships tallied throughout their entire careers are thirty-four for Nicklaus, Player, and Palmer; twenty-seven for Hagen, Hogan, and Sarazen; and seventeen for Vardon, Braid, and Taylor.

31 Wind, Foreword for Mackenzie, *Golf Architecture* (Reprint edition, The Classics of Golf, Ailsa, Inc., 1987), v.

32 Harold Hilton and Garden Smith, *The Royal and Ancient Game of Golf* (London: London and Counties Press, 1912).

33 Mark Frost, *The Greatest Game Ever Played: Harry Vardon, Francis Ouimet, and the Birth of Modern Golf* (New York: Hyperion, 2002), 475.

34 Peale, *The Power of Positive Thinking* (New York: Simon and Schuster, 1952).

35 Adams, *Watership Down* (London: Rex Collins, 1972). "Silflay" is a word from Adams's invented rabbit language, Lapine, which means "to go above ground to feed." Rabbits do this early in the morning and late in the afternoon, perfectly timed to encounter lone golfers.

36 Saying attributed to Ben Sayers (1856–1924), one of golf's most successful

early golf professionals. In addition to his career as a player, the wee Scotsman (only five feet three) was a highly regarded instructor, club maker, and golf course architect. His hand-forged "Benny" putter with its square-edged grip was a great innovation. The golf equipment company he founded in 1877 in North Berwick, Scotland, is the oldest such company still existing in the world, although its manufacturing headquarters moved to China in 2003. The many famous clients of Ben Sayers & Sons include Jack Nicklaus, who used a Sayers blade putter for years.

[37]   Invented in 1935 by Edward Stimpson, a fine amateur player and former captain of the Harvard golf team, the Stimpmeter is a device that measures green speeds. Initially made of wood, and now aluminum, it consists of a three-foot-long angled track that releases a ball at a consistent velocity so that the distance it rolls on a green's surface can be measured. The longer the roll on a flat surface, the faster the green. The United States Golf Association recommends that the normal Stimpmeter reading for a "fast" green is eight and a half feet; for the U.S. Open, ten and a half feet.

[38]   Minute Book of "The Gentlemen Golfers," *Articles & Laws in Playing at Golf,* March 7, 1744. Rule No. 7: "At Holling, you are to play your Ball honestly for the Hole, and, not to play upon your Adversary's Ball, not lying in your way to the Hole."

[39]   United States Golf Association and Royal and Ancient Rules Limited, *Rules of Golf and the Rules of Amateur Status,* 33rd Edition (R&A Limited and USGA, 2015), 29.

[40]   Sorenstam, *Golf Annika's Way: How I Elevated My Game to Be the Best – and How You Can, Too* (New York: Penguin, 2004).

[41]   Michael Freeman, "The 11 Levels of Irish Rain," *The Daily Edge* (January 21, 2014).

[42]   Thoreau, *Waldon Pond* (Boston: Ticknor and Fields, 1854).

[43]   Three examples of one-line *haiku* by John Wills:
"I catch the maple leaf   then let it go"
"the sun lights up a distant ridge   another"
"dusk   from rock to rock a waterthrush"

[44]   Similar plaques commemorate the site of Arnold Palmer's thrashed six-iron out of deep rough and a blackberry bush to the green on the fifteenth hole in the final round at Royal Birkdale for his Open victory in 1961; Tom Watson's seven-iron to two feet on the seventy-second hole at Turnberry to secure his win over Jack Nicklaus in their famous "Duel in the Sun" for the 1977 Open Championship; and a bronze tablet affixed to a rock adjacent to the eleventh tee at Merion, marking the completion of Bobby Jones's Grand Slam in 1930 on that hole with his victory in the U.S. Amateur.

INDEX